Queen Boudicca's
Battle of Britain

QUEEN BOUDICCA'S BATTLE OF BRITAIN

by

Richard Hunt

SPELLMOUNT
Staplehurst

British Library Cataloguing in Publication Data:
A catalogue record for this book is available
from the British Library

Copyright © Richard Hunt 2003

ISBN 1-86227-194-1

First published in the UK in 2003 by
Spellmount Limited
The Old Rectory
Staplehurst
Kent TN12 0AZ

Tel: 01580 893730
Fax: 01580 893731
E-mail: enquiries@spellmount.com
Website: www.spellmount.com

1 3 5 7 9 8 6 4 2

Typeset in Palatino by MATS, Southend-on-Sea, Essex
Printed in Great Britain by
TJ International Ltd, Padstow, Cornwall

Contents

List of Maps

List of Plates

Acknowledgements

Excerpts from Dio Cassius: Volumes VII and VIII – Roman History, The Loeb Classical Library 175 and 176, translated by Earnest Cary, are reprinted with the kind permission of Harvard University Press, Cambridge, MA, USA. The Loeb Classical Library is a registered trademark of the President and Fellows of Harvard College.

Excerpts from the following four works are reprinted with the kind permission of The Penguin Group, 80 Strand, London: *The Histories* by Tacitus, translated by Kenneth Wellesley (Penguin Classics 1964, revised edition 1975), copyright © Kenneth Wellesley 1964, 1972; *On Britain and Germany* by Tacitus, translated by H Mattingly (Penguin Classics 1948), copyright © The Estate of H Mattingly 1948; *Annals of Imperial Rome* by Tacitus, translated by Michael Grant (Penguin Classics 1956, sixth revised edition 1989), copyright © Michael Grant Publications Ltd 1956, 1989; *The Conquest of Gaul* by Julius Caesar, translated by S A Handford (Penguin Classics 1951, revised edition 1982), copyright the Estate of S A Handford 1951. Revisions copyright © Jane F Gardner 1982.

Excerpts from *The Twelve Caesars* by Suetonius, translated by Robert Graves (Penguin Classics 1957, reprinted with a new Bibliography 1989), copyright © Robert Graves 1957, are reprinted with the kind permission of the Carcanet Press Limited, 4th Floor, Conavon Court, 12–16 Blackfriars Street, Manchester M3 5BQ.

The author wishes to thank the following for their kind permission to reproduce some of the photographs in this book: Colchester Castle Museum (plates 1, 2, 3, 4, 5 and 16a); Iceni Village, Cockley Cley, Swaffham, Norfolk (plates 6 and 7); Lincoln and County Museum (plates 12b, 13 and 16b); Norwich Castle Museum (plates 10, 11 and 12a); Shrewsbury Museum (plates 14 and 15); J Smallwood and P Ovington for the use of photographs from their private collections.

In addition, I would like to thank David Hillier for his help in preparing the maps used in this book.

Richard Hunt
King's Lynn
February 2003

CHAPTER I

Introduction

You might think that accounts of the Roman invasion of Britain in AD43, and Queen Boudicca's rebellion of AD60 have been done to death by now, and that there cannot possibly be anything new to interest a reader. Well, in that case, you might be in for a surprise.

Have you ever read the actual words of the Roman historians who are the real source of all that is known about those events? You can hardly be blamed if you haven't. They lie scattered among the dry and dusty pages of several volumes which are primarily concerned with the activities of ancient Rome and its emperors. You need not search through those old books for them now. All the words from those ancient writers which relate to events in Britain from AD43 until about AD62, have been collected together in this volume, in as near as is possible to their correct chronological order.

The result, surprisingly enough, reads rather like a collection of journals or diaries that might have been kept by eye-witness observers nearly two thousand years ago. It is also anything but dry and dusty, because those authors were some of the best writers of their day, and knew well how to hold their audience and tell a good story. There is, though, a mild warning. This is all source material which is utterly unedited and un-censored by the red pens of modern historians – which means that it is you, not they, who must glean the truth, or as much of the truth as is possible, from their words.

Unravelling the ancient writers' stories is generally quite straight-forward, but that is not always the case. At times you might feel like a member of a jury struggling to make sense of the evidence in a murder trial. No doubt they wrote the truth as they saw it, but they were human, and problems arise when they contradict themselves, or express contra-dictory views. There are often gaps in their accounts too, which can only be tentatively bridged by a discussion of the possible options, and the judicious use of common-sense. But if you want to know what really happened nearly two thousand years ago, when the Romans invaded Britain, then it is well worth the effort.

I have made what I hope to be helpful comments, and where

1

appropriate have suggested alternative points of view for consideration, but I do not claim to have covered all the possibilities by any means.

A brief introduction to the ancient authors follows, and, to set the scene, there are two short chapters about the British and the Britain of AD43. Then the Roman invasion begins.

CHAPTER II

The Ancient Sources

Who were the ancient writers whose accounts we will be reading? Our main source of information on the period is the Roman historian Publius (or Gaius) Cornelius Tacitus, who was born in AD56 or 57, and died in about AD118. He most likely included British affairs in his books to the extent that he did simply because he married a daughter of Julius Agricola, who had been an officer in the occupying army at the time of Queen Boudicca's revolt, and who subsequently became the governor of Britain.

No doubt Tacitus learned a great deal about British affairs from Agricola, but he may also have known other old soldiers who had had first hand knowledge of events in these islands during the first century AD, and he may have had access to some of the official reports or documents in Rome's imperial archives.

There is a certain vagueness about Tacitus's origins His family *may* have come from the south of France, or from northern Italy. His father *may* have been an imperial agent at Trier or Cologne and paymaster-general for the armies on the Rhine. He was clearly a member of a provincial upper class family, and after a suitable education he ended up in Rome, where he embarked on a career as an official in the imperial civil service, and became a senator during the reign of the emperor Domitian.

Domitian was a tyrant, with many of the unpleasant characteristics of a Stalin or a Hitler, and like them much given to the purging of officials and others who he perceived might be a threat to his authority. At times he would compel the members of the Senate, including Tacitus presumably, to co-operate in his acts of tyranny by forcing them to denounce and condemn their own friends and colleagues to execution or enforced suicide. That Tacitus survived such a reign of terror might tell us something about his character and personality, but it is difficult to be quite sure what. Perhaps he was a yes-man, determined to hang on to his prestigious office regardless of how many of his friends he had to tread over and betray. On the other hand, to be faced with the alternatives of either publicly condoning injustices that he had no possible way of preventing, or losing his own life, should surely engender some sympathy from those of us who have never had to face such stark choices.

Nevertheless one wonders whether he was the type of person one would really want to introduce into one's own close circle of friends. Rome was obviously not the place to be in those days, and Tacitus, with his wife, who is unfortunately never named, somehow managed to get to a less dangerous place from at least AD89 until AD93, which was the year his father-in-law, Agricola, died.

From his career point of view, Tacitus had obviously done all the right things, for in AD97, the year after Domitian's death, he attained the highest metropolitan post – the consulship, and some fifteen years later became the governor of the great province of western Anatolia. So much for the progress of his career, which shows that he must have met all the right people, and been well aware of what was going on throughout the empire. He evidently studied under Rome's leading orators when he was a young man, for he became one of the best known speakers of his time, and it would appear that much of what he later wrote was intended to be 'declaimed', that is to say, to be read aloud.

Agricola died in AD93, but it was not until AD98 that Tacitus started his additional career as a historian, by publishing a semi-biographical work about his father-in-law, entitled simply *Agricola*. It is a scrappy sort of book, which starts off as though it was intended to be a history of Britain and the British, but then drifts into being a rather terse and over fulsome account of his father-in-law's term as governor. In that same year he wrote the *Germania*, which, as the name suggests, is a study of the tribes of northern and central Europe. It contains no references to Britain.

Tacitus's two principal works of Roman history came next. The first, *The Histories*, completed in about AD112, was intended to cover the period from AD68 onwards. The second, the *Annals of Imperial Rome* henceforth referred to simply as the *Annals*, covered Roman History from AD14 to the death of Nero. So from Tacitus we have two accounts of early British history, one in the *Agricola*, and the other in the *Annals*.

Tacitus would not rate highly as a modern historian. He may have accurately recorded events as he knew or had researched them, but far more often than not geographical locations, place names, times of year, and general military details are either inadequate or lacking entirely. There is little about Britain's trade, or social or economic structure, and almost nothing on the strategic positioning of the occupying forces.

Time has not improved the *Annals* – sections of it are missing, including, unfortunately, the part covering the Claudian invasion of Britain in AD43 and the first few years of Roman occupation. Frankly, it is surprising that any of Tacitus's works have survived that length of time. The surviving copies are medieval, and therefore are copies of earlier copies – so errors and omissions must be a real possibility.

There is another early Roman historian whose works also cover the period

4

we are interested in. Dio Cassius Cocceianus was in fact a Greek, and he was born in AD150, some thirty years or so after Tacitus's death. His father was the governor of the minor province of Cilicia. He must have been thoroughly romanised and fluent in Latin because in AD180, Dio, like Tacitus before him, went to Rome and eventually entered the Senate. He became a close friend of several emperors, and subsequently held high offices. He was at some time governor of Pergamum and Smyrna; consul; proconsul of Africa; governor of Dalmatia and later also of Pannonia; and consul again in AD229. He died in Nicaea in AD235.

His works on Roman history, which consisted originally of eighty books, were written in Greek, but some of those have also become lost in the passage of time. Fortunately, the ones relating to the early years of Rome's occupation of Britain survive. He was, of course, not con-temporaneous with that period, and unlike Tacitus, had no personal interest in Britain, so his accounts tend to be briefer in content. He almost certainly had access to Tacitus's works – some of his passages are too similarly worded for that not to have been the case, but he also had excellent opportunities for research into Rome's imperial archives. If his account of events differs from Tacitus's we must remember that Dio would have known that too, and it ought to be assumed that he had chosen his words carefully. Modern historians seem to prefer Tacitus's words to Dio's, but we should keep an open mind, and assess their reliability on specific points, when the occasion warrants it.

Tacitus and Dio are the main sources of our early British history, but there are a few relevant quotations about the Emperors Vespasian, Nero and Claudius, which come from a work entitled *The Twelve Caesars*, written by Gaius Suetonius Tranquillus, who was born in or about AD69, and subsequently wrote widely on all manner of other interesting subjects, which have, unfortunately, failed to survive.

Julius Caesar is the earliest significant source of information about Britain and the British, and so some of the passages in his *Conquest of Gaul* have been used as background material, even though they pre-date the period we are interested in.

It is important to remember, when considering the words of our sources, that they were all upper class Romans whose writings were intended to be read to, or by, others of the same ilk. Their society was male dominated, and slavery was an acceptable practice, as was the sight of death and slaughter in the gladiatorial arena. At times, and Tacitus particularly, they seem to express more liberal or sympathetic views on the plight of the native Britons, only for the illusion to disintegrate completely in the next callous sentence. They are also, for readers who are British, on the wrong side – the enemy's side; so the task of getting at a semblance of the truth might sometimes seem as difficult as having to put together the story of the 1940 aerial Battle of Britain over southern England, from accounts written twenty or thirty years later by German bomber or fighter pilots, who were also there.

These sources were not only written nearly two thousand years ago, they were written in Latin or Greek. Over the past few hundred years there must have been many translations into English, some, no doubt, better than others. The study of such languages is a highly specialised subject, and one would expect there to have occasionally been differences of opinion among scholars, but it has been assumed, I hope correctly, that by now any significant areas of controversy have long since been debated at length and ironed out into some sort of consensus of meaning. The most accessible English language editions are those published by Loeb Classical Library and Penguin Classics, and they probably offer the most accurate translations available.

It is time now to find out what Britain was like in AD43, the year the Romans invaded.

CHAPTER III
About Britain and the British circa AD43

What was Britain like nearly two thousand years ago in AD43, and what is known about its inhabitants?

The climate was not that much different from today's apparently. A trifle drier perhaps, but even so the heavier soils would certainly have been covered by forests as dense as nature left alone could make them. Even the lighter soils on the chalk downs would have supported a tangled scrub of birch, gorse, bracken and brambles. That would probably have been the picture generally all over the whole island, had it not been for the cumulative effects of several thousand years of human habitation.

There is no need to elaborate here on the changes that brought man, in these islands, as elsewhere, from being nomadic hunter-gatherers to more settled herdsmen and arable farmers, except to say the obvious, that when it happened it would have been easier for the chalk ridge scrub lands to be cleared for fields and grazing, rather than the forests. The chalk down lands have evidence enough, with their stone circles, barrows and tumuli, of a considerable population size, whose food production methods were good enough to provide an adequate source of nutritious energy, as well as the spare time for many of them to have become somewhat addicted to playing Lego with twenty-ton blocks of stone.

While subsistence was presumably that easy, there would have been only limited pressure to clear forested land and bring it into cultivation. They would certainly have wanted a healthy surplus of storable food to see them safely through the winter, or to the next harvest, or even to barter, but there would hardly have been production for production's sake. Only an increase in population would have forced that issue, but the very existence of a settled farm or community probably caused some local forest clearance in that area, since the demand for timber, both as a building material and as a fuel, would probably have outstripped natural regeneration. Also, once a definitive edge had been formed to a wood then high winds and gales would from time to time uproot and fell more of the trees, and grazing animals might have prevented sapling regrowth. So additional land may have become available for cultivation without the need for large-scale slash and burn activity.

We can reasonably assume that such homesteads or communities were generally sited on firm, dry ground, and as near a good water supply as was possible. Paths or tracks would have made communications between settlements within the same or adjacent river valleys relatively easy, but to have ventured farther afield into the untamed forest would have been fraught with danger. That would still have been the home of wolves and bears, and the human traveller would have had them to contend with, as well as those of his own kind who might have felt threatened by the sudden appearance of strangers in their territory. If one had a need to travel in those early days, then it would have been wiser and safer to avoid the forests, and get onto the more populated grassy chalk downs and ridges. There are plenty of those in the south and east of Britain. They sweep south from Yorkshire and the Lincolnshire Wolds, across what is now the Wash, through Norfolk, Cambridgeshire and Hertfordshire, then west through Berkshire to Salisbury Plain and the West Country, and south-east to Hampshire, Surrey, Sussex and Kent. On those ridges are found the earliest track ways.

They would have needed little adaptation to meet the needs of the mounted or on-foot traveller, or the drivers of cattle, even though repeated undulations from hill top to valley floor, and back to hill top again, might have tested the leg muscles somewhat, but that would have been preferable to the dangers, swamps, bogs and denser undergrowth of the lower contours. When traders or tinker craftsmen appeared, pack-horses would probably have carried their weighty goods or tools, but around 1500BC wheeled transport came to Britain. A simple cart-like structure, drawn by a horse or two, or even by a man or two, would have been able to carry the loads of many pack animals, but wheels have disadvantages. It would have been hard work trying to drag carts straight up and down the slopes of those chalky ridges, so subtle changes would have been made to the original ancient routes by cutting out some of the worst gradients and following instead, where possible, the contour lines of the hills.

This was when the branch of civil engineering known as road building probably began, albeit in a haphazard fashion. A few hacks with a reindeer antler pick may have started the track along a contour line; a few holes filled in with loose stones, bracken, branches and logs to firm up a swampy bit. All these, repeated often enough over the years would have created something akin to a road. It wasn't just haphazard changes though. In some places specific working parties seem to have been organised to make log or 'corduroy' roads through particularly marshy areas, some sections of which still remain to delight the archaeologist. These were sometimes made up of four- to six-inch girders of fir and alder, laid in the direction of the road. On those might be placed a thick layer of secured osiers and twigs, topped by cross-pieces or 'sleepers' of three-inch pine to lock and peg it all together. Then it might be finished off with a compacted surface of beaten clay.

In addition to roads, in those areas served by river networks there would almost certainly have been a movement of goods and people from place to place by water transport consisting of rafts, barges and boats, and evidence of wooden piled wharves for loading and unloading sometimes survives to give credence to the obvious.

So much for generalities. It is now time to read the observations of Julius Caesar, who actually saw things in early Britain for himself. He wrote in about 54BC but things probably did not change significantly for Britain's inhabitants in the next hundred years. In *The Conquest of Gaul*, Caesar writes:

> *The interior of Britain . . . is inhabited by people who claim, on the strength of an oral tradition, to be aboriginal* [of an indigenous native race], *the coasts by Belgic immigrants who came to plunder and make war – nearly all of them retaining the names of the tribes from which they originated – and later settled down to till the soil. The population is exceedingly large, the ground thickly studded with homesteads, closely resembling those of the Gauls, and the cattle very numerous. For money they use either bronze, or gold coins, or iron ingots of fixed weights. Tin is found inland, and small quantities of iron near the coast; the copper that they use is imported. There is timber of every kind, as in Gaul, except beech and fir. Hares, fowl, and geese they think it unlawful to eat, but rear them for pleasure and amusement. The climate is more temperate than in Gaul, the cold being less severe.*

Tacitus, in his *Agricola*, also comments on the British weather.

> *The climate is objectionable, with its frequent rains and mists, but there is no extreme cold. Their day is longer than is normal in the Roman world. The night is bright and, in the extreme North, short, with only a brief interval between evening and morning twilight. If no clouds block the view, the sun's glow, it is said, can be seen all night long. It does not set and rise, but simply passes along the horizon. The reason must be that the ends of the earth, being flat, cast low shadows and cannot raise the darkness to any height; night therefore fails to reach the sky and its stars.*

That last sentence is quite fascinating. We are not familiar, these days, with the ramifications of a 'flat-earth' concept, and the problems that resulted when trying to explain natural phenomena. Tacitus continues:

> *The soil can bear all produce, except the olive, the vine, and other natives of warmer climes, and it is fertile. Crops are slow to ripen, but quick to grow –*

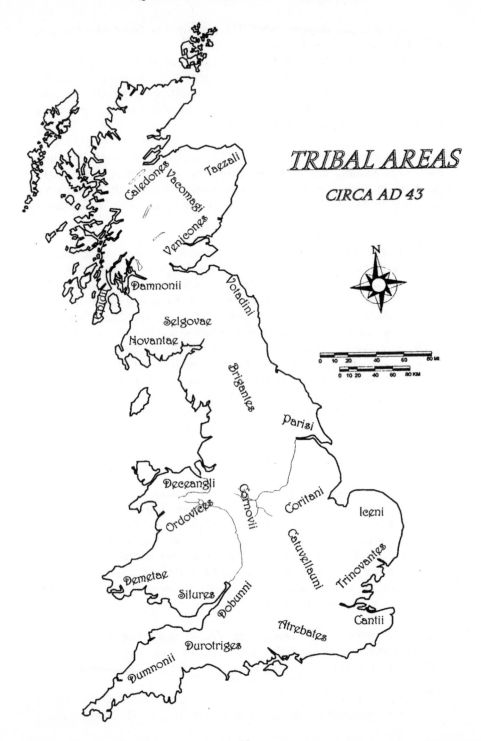

TRIBAL AREAS

CIRCA AD 43

both facts due to one and the same cause, the extreme moistness of land and sky. Britain yields gold, silver and other metals, to make it worth conquering. Ocean, too, has its pearls, but they are dusky and mottled. Some think that the natives are unskilled in gathering them. Whereas in the Red Sea the oysters are torn alive and breathing from the rocks, in Britain they are collected as the sea throws them up. I find it easier to believe in a defect of quality in the pearls than of greed in us.

What Tacitus means in that last sentence is not at all clear. It may be a copyist's error; for what on earth could Roman greed have to do with cloudy pearls?

Julius Caesar has something to say about Britain's inhabitants:

By far the most civilised inhabitants are those living in Kent (a purely maritime district), whose way of life differs little from that of the Gauls. Most of the tribes in the interior do not grow corn but live on milk and meat, and wear skins. All the Britons dye their bodies with woad, which produces a blue colour, and this gives them a more terrifying appearance in battle. They wear their hair long, and shave the whole of their bodies except the head and the upper lip. Wives are shared between groups of ten or twelve men, especially between brothers and between fathers and sons; but the offspring of these unions are counted as the children of the man with whom a particular woman cohabited first.

Caesar may have been confusing 'wives' with female slaves or concubines, for certainly the Britons also had more conventional relationships. He mentions their marriage contracts in a later passage.

Tacitus, writing over one hundred years later, had some very interesting things to say about the populace, again from his *Agricola*.

Who the first inhabitants of Britain were, whether natives or immigrants, remains obscure; one must remember we are dealing with barbarians. But physical characteristics vary, and that very variation is suggestive. The reddish hair and large limbs of the Caledonians [the Scots] proclaim a German origin, the swarthy faces of the Silures [a South Wales tribe], the tendency of their hair to curl and the fact that Spain lies opposite, all lead one to believe that Spaniards crossed in ancient times and occupied the land. The peoples nearest to the Gauls are correspondingly like them. Perhaps the original strain persists, perhaps it is climatic conditions that determine physical type in lands that converge from opposite directions on a single point. On a general estimate, however, we may believe that it was Gauls who took possession of the neighbouring island.

Those brief descriptions of the Welsh and the Highlander Scot are still

11

recognisable characteristics of some of the people living in those areas today. Yet the school books told us that the inhabitants of Wales and Scotland were driven into those mountainous regions from England by waves of foreign invaders, starting with the Romans, but that cannot be entirely correct, since Tacitus here clearly states that in his time some of those people were already there.

Caesar now comments on the structure of society in Gaul – which is probably also relevant to Britain. From what he says not a great deal has changed in that respect either.

> *Everywhere in Gaul there are only two classes of men who are of any account or consideration. The common people are treated almost as slaves, never venture to act on their own initiative, and are not consulted on any subject. Most of them, crushed by debts or heavy taxation or the oppression of more powerful persons, bind themselves to serve men of rank, who exercise over them all the rights that masters have over slaves. The two privileged classes are the Druids and the Knights.*

Back to Tacitus, also on the subject of our ancestors, in the *Agricola*:

> *But the Britons show more spirit; they have not yet been softened by protracted peace. The Gauls, too, we have been told, had their hour of military glory; but then came decadence with peace, and valour went the way of lost liberty. The same fate has befallen such of the Britons as have long been conquered; the rest are still what the Gauls used to be. ... The Britons themselves submit to the levy, the tribute and the other charges of Empire with cheerful readiness, provided that there is no abuse. That they bitterly resent; for they are broken in to obedience, not to slavery.*

Now we learn about those two classes of so-called really important people – the Druids and the Knights. The Druids first. Again, although Caesar was writing specifically about the Druids of Gaul, his remarks clearly also apply to the Druids of Britain. Caesar may have found them to have been particularly interesting people, for he writes about them at considerable length, but perhaps they were not so numerous or as influential as he suggests, because other Roman writers hardly mention them.

> *The Druids officiate at the worship of the gods, regulate public and private sacrifices, and give rulings on all religious questions. Large numbers of young men flock to them for instruction, and they are held in great honour by the people. They act as judges in practically all disputes, whether between tribes or between individuals; when any crime is committed, or a murder takes place, or a dispute arises about an inheritance or a boundary, it is they who adjudicate the matter and appoint the compensation to be paid and*

received by the parties concerned. Any individual or tribe failing to accept
their award is banned from taking part in sacrifice – the heaviest punishment
that can be inflicted upon a Gaul. Those who are laid under such a ban are
regarded as impious criminals. Everyone shuns them and avoids going near
or speaking to them, for fear of taking some harm by contact with what is
unclean; if they appear as plaintiffs, justice is denied them, and they are
excluded from a share in any honour.

All the Druids are under one head, whom they hold in the highest respect.
On his death, if any one of the rest is of outstanding merit, he succeeds to the
vacant place; if several have equal claims, the Druids usually decide the
election by voting, though sometimes they actually fight it out. On a fixed
date in each year they hold a session in a consecrated spot in the country of
the Carnutes, which is supposed to be the centre of Gaul. Those who are
involved in disputes assemble here from all parts, and accept the Druids'
judgements and awards. The Druidic doctrine is believed to have been found
existing in Britain and thence imported into Gaul; even today those who
want to make a profound study of it generally go to Britain for the purpose.

The Druids are exempt from military service and do not pay taxes like
other citizens. These important privileges are naturally attractive, many
present themselves of their own accord to become students of Druidism, and
others are sent by their parents or relatives. It is said that these pupils have
to memorise a great number of verses – so many, that some of them spend
twenty years at their studies. The Druids believe that their religion forbids
them to commit their teachings to writing, although for most other purposes,
such as public and private accounts, the Gauls use the Greek alphabet. But I
imagine that this rule was originally established for other reasons – because
they did not want their doctrine to become public property, and in order to
prevent their pupils from relying on the written word and neglecting to train
their memories; for it is usually found that when people have the help of texts,
they are less diligent in learning by heart, and let their memories rust. A
lesson which they take particular pains to inculcate is that the soul does not
perish, but after death passes from one body to another; they think that this
is the best incentive to bravery, because it teaches men to disregard the
terrors of death. They also hold long discussions about the heavenly bodies
and their movements, the size of the universe and of the earth, the physical
constitution of the world, and the power and properties of the gods; and they
instruct the young men in all these subjects.

Having read all that about a wealth of ancient knowledge, one wonders if
that was the real source of the learning claimed by the classical Greek
mathematicians and philosophers. If the Druids used the Greek alphabet
for mundane matters there must have been cultural exchanges of some
sort with Greece. Did those now famous Greek mathematicians and
scholars merely write down some of the Druids' ancient secret

knowledge, and thus claim, or cause posterity to attribute, the Druidic teachings as their own inventions?

There is no mention of the Druids giving medical treatment, except for arranging life-saving sacrifices, or of them forecasting the future, or indeed, relating epic warrior sagas to lyre music for entertainment purposes. Perhaps Caesar omitted to mention them, but perhaps the Druids cannot be directly compared, as some would have us do, to 'witch-doctors', mushroom-eating soothsayers, or even the travelling bards prevalent in myth and legend.

Tacitus may go on about barbarians being the lowest of the low, but Caesar seems to be describing the Druids as a sophisticated, deeply intellectual society, with a strong Cambridge and Oxford-like base of learning and knowledge.

So much for the Druids. Next, the Knights:

> *The second class is that of the Knights. When their services are required in some war that has broken out – and before Caesar's arrival in the country the Gallic states used to fight offensive or defensive wars almost every year – these all take the field, surrounded by their servants and retainers, of whom each Knight has a great number according to his birth and fortune. The possession of such a following is the only criterion of position and power that they recognise.*

Next Caesar comments on some of the general beliefs and customs.

> *As a nation the Gauls are extremely superstitious; and so persons suffering from serious diseases, as well as those who are exposed to the perils of battle, offer, or vow to offer, human sacrifices, for the performance of which they employ Druids. They believe that the only way of saving a man's life is to propitiate the god's wrath by rendering another life in its place, and they have regular state sacrifices of the same kind. Some tribes have colossal images made of wickerwork, the limbs of which they fill with living men; they are then set on fire, and the victims burnt to death. They think that the gods prefer the execution of men taken in the act of theft or brigandage, or guilty of some offence; but when they run short of criminals, they do not hesitate to make up with innocent men.*
>
> *The god they reverence most is Mercury. They have very many images of him, and regard him as the inventor of all arts, the god who directs men upon their journeys, and their most powerful helper in trading and getting money. Next to him they reverence Apollo, Mars, Jupiter and Minerva, about whom they have much the same ideas as other nations – that Apollo averts illness, and Minerva teaches the principles of industries and handicrafts; that Jupiter is king of the gods, and Mars the lord of war. When they have decided to fight a battle they generally vow to Mars the booty that they hope to take,*

and after a victory they sacrifice the captured animals and collect the rest of the spoil in one spot. Among many of the tribes, high piles of it can be seen on consecrated ground; and it is an almost unknown thing for anyone to dare, in defiance of religious law, to conceal his booty at home or to remove anything placed on the piles. Such a crime is punishable by a terrible death under torture.

It is interesting to note that Caesar makes no mention of a 'mother goddess', or the desire for the constant 'fertility' sacrifices that we are often led to believe dominated the minds of early societies.

The Gauls claim all to be descended from Father Dis, declaring that this is the tradition preserved by the Druids. For this reason they measure periods of time not by days but by nights; and in celebrating birthdays, the first of the month, and new year's day, they go on the principle that the day begins at night. As regards the other usages of daily life, the chief difference between them and other peoples is that their children are not allowed to go up to their fathers in public until they are old enough for military service; they regard it as unbecoming for a son who is still a boy to stand in his father's sight in a public place.

When a Gaul marries, he adds to the dowry that his wife brings with her a portion of his own property estimated to be of equal value. A joint account is kept of the whole amount, and the profits which it earns are put aside; and when either dies, the survivor receives both shares together with the accumulated profits. Husbands have power of life and death over their wives as well as their children. When a high-born head of a family dies, his relatives assemble, and if the circumstances of his death are suspicious, they examine his widow under torture, as we examine slaves; if her guilt is established, she is consigned to the flames and put to death with the most cruel torments. Gallic funerals are splendid and costly, for a comparatively poor country. Everything that the dead man is supposed to have been fond of, including even animals, is placed upon his pyre, and not long ago there were people still alive who could remember the time when slaves and retainers known to have been beloved by their masters were burnt with them at the conclusion of the funeral rites.

The tribes which are considered to manage their affairs best have a law that if anyone hears from a neighbouring country any rumour or news that concerns the state, he is to communicate it to a magistrate without speaking of it to anyone else. For experience has shown that impulsive and ignorant persons are often frightened by false reports into subversive action, and meddle with important affairs of state. The magistrates suppress what they think it advisable to keep secret, and publish only what they deem it expedient for the people to know. The discussion of politics is forbidden except in a public assembly.

The techniques of government were obviously well known even in those days. Our sources have now finished expounding on general social activities. This is what they have to say on military matters. Caesar:

> In chariot fighting the Britons begin by driving all over the field hurling javelins, and generally the terror inspired by the horses and the noise of the wheels is sufficient to throw their opponents' ranks into disorder. Then, after making their way between the squadrons of their own cavalry, they jump down from the chariots and engage on foot. In the meantime their charioteers retire a short distance from the battle and place the chariots in such a position that their masters, if hard pressed by numbers, have an easy means of retreat to their own lines. Thus they combine the mobility of cavalry with the staying power of infantry, and by daily training and practice they attain such proficiency that even on a steep incline they are able to control the horses at full gallop, and to check and turn them in a moment. They can run along the chariot pole, stand on the yoke, and get back into the chariot as quick as lightning.

This last sentence of Caesar's is almost identical to an account of the chariot-borne antics of the Thracians in Alexander the Great's army. The use of chariots in warfare had died out in Europe since Alexander's day, except, it seems, in Britain, and their appearance against Caesar's troops in 55BC appears to have engendered some surprise, and the above little sketch. The chariots would certainly have interested Caesar, since he was a fan of Alexander. He may have been a fan of Homer too, and have seen these outmoded weapon systems enacting the same tactical manoeuvres that the Greeks and Trojans had used over a thousand years earlier. Tacitus also has a little to say in the *Agricola* on the subject of fighting in Britain.

> Their strength is in their infantry. Some tribes also fight from chariots. The nobleman drives, his dependants fight in his defence. Once they owed obedience to kings; now they are distracted between the jarring factions of rival chiefs. Indeed, nothing has helped us more in war with their strongest nations than their inability to co-operate. It is but seldom that two or three states unite to repel a common danger; fighting in detail they are conquered wholesale.

Next Tacitus and Caesar give us some geographical information about Britain's size, shape and position relative to the mainland of Europe. For the benefit of students of historical cartography, if there are any, these accounts are given in full in the Appendix. What they say is of general interest, and excites speculation about the methods used in those pre-compass, sextant, and aerial photography days, to come up with any kind of charts or maps, but they do not add anything to our knowledge of the history of this island. Which is a great pity. A really good map of Britain circa AD60 would probably have given us, in a single glance, the solution to a serious geographical problem.

The coast line of Britain now, because of the effects of sea level changes and erosion, is obviously considerably different to what it was then. Normally such changes would not have any significant effect on historical events in these relatively geologically stable islands, but that is not the case for the period we are interested in. The tribe which rebelled under Queen Boudicca's leadership in AD60 was the Iceni, who occupied present day Norfolk. In order to properly understand what may have happened then we need to be sure we understand Norfolk's geography at that date, and how it related to the rest of Britain.

To the north of that county is the Wash, to the west are the Fens, and to the east is the North Sea. So, before the Fens were drained a few hundred years ago, it would seem that most of Norfolk was effectively cut off from the rest of Britain in all directions other than from the south. It was a place, apparently, that was on the way to nowhere.

Yet two ancient roads pass through west Norfolk. The oldest – the Icknield Way – is a prehistoric trackway which follows the chalk ridges all the way from the south and the west of England, through Hertfordshire, Cambridgeshire, Newmarket, and on to Norfolk, where it disappears into the Wash not far from Hunstanton. The other is a Roman road which is called the Peddars Way, and that runs north from Colchester, through Suffolk and into Norfolk, where it also gets onto the same chalk ridge as the Icknield Way, and it too disappears into the Wash at much the same place.

About ten miles away, on the other side of the Wash, in Lincolnshire, not far from Skegness, an un-named Roman road appears out of the sea, together with the much older Icknield Way, and both head northish along what is the geological continuation of the Norfolk Edge chalk ridge, but which is there known as the Lincolnshire Wolds. The Icknield Way then heads northward to the Humber and Yorkshire, while the Roman road swings westward, to pass just a little to the north of Lincoln, and then goes on to York via Doncaster.

The few history books that bother to mention these roads, merely suggest that there may once have been a ferry linking them across the Wash. That may be true, but it is not a very satisfactory explanation. The Wash is a treacherous stretch of choppy water at the best of times, with strong currents and a prevailing easterly wind ready to cast the unwary sailor onto a lee shore. It is also difficult to imagine nomadic neolithic or bronze age travellers with their flocks and herds patiently waiting for a ferry to come and take them across. As for the Romans, well, their roads were meant to allow for the rapid passage of troops in an emergency, and how quickly could a Roman legion, with all its gear, be moved across several miles of unpredictable sea? The suggestion that a large number of naval vessels may have been kept there permanently, waiting for just such an eventuality, does not sound very credible.

Perhaps Peddars Way was only a very minor road, and not intended for bulk or hurried transport. If the width of the *agger* – that is to say the raised platform created by the material used in the roads' construction – is anything to go by, then Peddars Way, which varies from 36ft to 45ft, is generally wider than the prime arterial Roman roads of Watling Street (approximately 33ft), and Ermine Street (approximately 30ft), and it is built to at least the same, if not to a higher specification. So, rather than being a minor road, it must have been a major one. In simple economic terms, although the Romans may have used forced labour to do the heavy work, its construction must have been a major investment in both time and money. It may also have been built early in their occupation period, when there was much else for them to do.

If the Wash was not there, we would all readily accept that Peddars Way was once a major trunk road linking Colchester with Lincoln and the north. Yet those old roads are factual. They cannot be ignored or mentally put to one side just because we cannot readily understand their purpose.

Perhaps we need to look at things from a different point of view, and question whether the Wash in ancient times was the barrier to road transport that it is now. Perhaps the ferry journey was then only a short one, or perhaps the Wash was once even fordable.

Trying to find the answers to those questions means dabbling tentatively into the preserves of the geologist, and one soon learns that both the Wash and the Fens are areas of extreme geological complexity. However, there is one thing that is not in doubt, the chalk hills of the Lincolnshire Wolds are definitely a geological continuation of the chalk hills of north-west Norfolk. So in the far distant past it would certainly have been possible to walk along them dry shod from Norfolk into Lincolnshire. When then did the Wash come into being?

One authority holds that the eastwards flowing rivers first breached the chalk hills in the Wash area during the Tertiary period. Other authorities believe that the whole of the Fen basin was excavated by ice during one of the Quaternary cold phases. Either way, the rivers that now have their estuaries in the Wash would then have flowed into what was probably a vast lake or marsh covering the Fen basin. River-borne silts would have been deposited there, and if the excess water did not flow out through the Humber, as it may once have done, then it would have flowed over the chalk ridge, through the then dry land of today's North Sea, to enter the Atlantic Ocean somewhere near Scotland.

There were more cold spells to come, and the ice' of subsequent glaciation must have stilled the flow of water and prevented anyone walking the chalk ridge.

Twelve thousand years ago, at the end of the Devensian glaciation, the southern part of the North Sea was still dry land all the way to continental Europe. In about 7600BC the sea broke through the Straights of Dover. A thousand years later the sea had risen high enough to flood the East Anglian side of the southern North Sea, and Britain became an island.

From that point in time the new coastline of Britain became exposed to tides and currents, and promptly started to erode. Obviously chalky and other soft cliff formations eroded faster than harder rocks. Parts of the chalky West Sussex coast have, it has been estimated, retreated at the astonishing rate of some 4.5 to 6.0 metres per year, or a total of 9km–12km (5–7 miles) since AD43. Studies have also shown that since Roman times sea levels may have risen in places by as much as 4 metres (13 feet).

I have found no such estimates relating specifically to the Wash, but if the Sussex rates of erosion applied similarly to each of the relevant cliffs of Lincolnshire and of Norfolk, then in AD43 the Wash would obviously have been dramatically narrower. Adjusting for sea level changes, though, is not so simple, because modern charts show that there are some relatively narrow channels that are up to 25 metres deep. They may have been dredged to allow shipping access to Boston and King's Lynn, or simply be the natural scouring effect of river flow, but how one could estimate what depth they were nearly two thousand years ago, I do not know. However, the Wash generally is relatively shallow, and lowering the sea level by 4 metres would certainly bring a vast area back into dryish land. So both adjustments effectively reduce the width of the Wash, perhaps to the size of a large river estuary.

If the mind can adjust to the mental picture of a wide, perhaps sluggish, estuary, with an area of salt-marsh and muddy creeks on both sides, full of sea birds when exposed at low tide, the whole question of a practicable, even fordable, crossing takes on a lot more credence. One can visualise prehistoric man building log causeways over parts of the marshes to make the going easier, and even erecting simple bridges to span some of the deeper channels.

The Romans, with their technological expertise, would, no doubt, have done even better. Caesar built a bridge over the Rhine, so perhaps something similar was constructed here. Four main rivers still make their entry to the sea in the Wash – the Witham, the Welland, the Nene and the Great Ouse. The first two probably combined not far from Boston. Until the 11th century the Great Ouse apparently flowed through Wisbech, where it probably joined the Nene, but whether they were all united before joining the sea, is mere speculation, but we ought to assume they were, because the Romans did not use the name Wash for this area. They called it the Metaris estuary.

At this point it may be of interest to refer to what is known as Ptolemy's map, which was apparently created from co-ordinates given in a book

ISLE OF
MAN

R. Mersey

R. Dee

Humber

Metaris Estuary
(The Wash)

Thames Estuary

Bristol Channel

ISLE OF
WIGHT

THE COASTLINE OF BRITAIN
PTOLEMY'S MAP
2nd Century AD

called *Geography*, written in the 2nd century AD. It looks very crude, but the main features of the British coastline, such as the Thames and Severn estuaries, and the Isles of Wight and Man are easily identifiable, but the Wash as we know it, is not. It is shown as being much narrower from north to south, and Lincolnshire bulges far out into the North Sea. Taking into account sea levels and erosion, that tends to confirm what we ought to expect, but this is clearly not a document that one can use with any confidence.

The flow of water through the Metaris estuary may not have been vastly different to that of the Thames, which was itself fordable at some unknown place downstream from London, where Dio Cassius will later tell us the Britons crossed '. . . at a point where it empties into the ocean, and at flood-tide forms a lake'. The Humber was apparently fordable too, not far from the present Humber bridge, but the most compelling reason for believing that the Metaris estuary may have been fordable, or at least relatively easily crossed in AD60, is surely the belief that the Romans would never have undertaken the construction of Peddars Way if it had not been – and neither would the Icknield Way ever have become an important prehistoric trackway.

So, and this is the main point, Norfolk was probably not isolated and cut off from the rest of Britain, because through it may have passed the main Roman road from Colchester to Lincoln and the north.

That is as good a place as any to leave the question of whether there was a ford or a ferry, but something else of interest came to light while delving into the geological complexity of the Fens and the Wash – which might affect our mental picture of what the landscape of that particular area was like in Roman times.

It was in a very old book entitled simply *Lost England*, written by a man named Beckles Willson. From this I learned that some large tracts of land in Britain had suddenly become submerged in ancient times. The part of Cornwall once known by the name of Lyonesse was possibly inundated at the same time as the Lowland hundred in Cardigan Bay, the latter apparently being described by Welsh chroniclers, but what was of much more interest to me was the suggestion that there had also been a similar inundation in and around the Fens and the Wash.

> *There can also be no doubt that the destruction of the country was occasioned by an irruption of the sea. The theory of Stukely and Dugdale deserves to be mentioned. They opine that the event was the result of an earthquake which, by lowering the level of the land several feet, exposed it to the inroads of the sea. It is probable that this same cause has operated elsewhere on our coasts, to account for the sudden submersion of vast tracts by the sea. Dugdale's remarks cannot fail to be of interest: 'That the vast level of the Fens was at first a firm, dry land, and not annoyed with any extraordinary inundation*

from the sea, I shall now endeavour to make manifest ... In Marshland, about a mile westwards from Magdalen Bridge, at the setting down of a sluice very lately, there was discovered at 17 feet deep, divers furze bushes, as also nut trees pressed flat down, with nuts sound and firm lying by them ... the ocean broke into it with great violence, as that the woods then standing throughout the same became turned up by the roots; and so great a portion of silt brought in as did cover the ground in an extraordinary depth, even to the remotest parts on the verge of the highlands.'

That seemed a little too dramatic to be believable at first, but the book had more to add on the same lines.

Near Bardney, only 8 miles east of Lincoln and 20 miles from the coast, about 3 feet down ...

'on which bed was found a large number of oak, yew, and alder roots and trees, which had grown thereon. The soil on each side is moory and full of subterranean wood, up to three and a half feet thick.' This moor stratum is usually about a foot thick; upon and within it one found stags' horns, warlike instruments, and other remains of the ancient inhabitants. In Friskney, Wainfleet and Wrangle, and in the East Fen, great numbers of fir trees, with their roots, have been discovered lying in the moory soil ... Again, at the laying of a new sluice at the fall of Hammond Beck into Boston haven, in taking up the foundation of the old gowt, they met with the roots of trees which, when removed with the surrounding black earth, disclosed a gravelly, stony soil, similar to that of the high country, and beyond question the surface of the lost country.

So whole forests were suddenly flattened at some point in time, but there was something much more interesting than trees.

At the laying of Skynbeck sluice, near Boston, there was found, sixteen feet deep, covered with silt, a smith's forge and 'all the tools thereunto belonging'.

Clearly then, a whole area had once been subjected to a catastrophe of major proportions. The sudden subsidence of a large area of land might have been followed by a sizeable *tsunami* or tidal wave, which may have uprooted all those trees. More modern geomorphologists than those Beckles Willson has quoted, have stated that the smith's forge found at Skynbeck sluice was a Roman one, and that the inundation actually took place in the 4th century AD.

The Fenland Survey (1994) explains one of the reasons why subsidence may have occurred in the area. It is worded in a precise and technical way, but its meaning is clear enough. Unconsolidated sediments up to 100 feet thick had accumulated in places in the Fenland and western Wash region during the previous 10,000 years. From time to time those sediments may have compacted. Compaction here means the lowering of relative height by a reduction in volume caused by the upward movement, or upwards release of pore fluids or water. The degree of such compaction varies with the grain size of the sediment type. Peat layers can be reduced to only 10% of their original thickness, clayey muds to 11–25%, calcite muds to 50%, and sands to 66–75%.

Although compaction of sediments may have occurred in places at various times during the past 10,000 years, it would seem that in the 4th century AD there may have been one over a relatively large area of south Lincolnshire and north Cambridgeshire. An earth tremor may certainly have triggered such an event, and created a *tsunami* big enough to uproot all those trees.

However, this inundation may not have been restricted to those areas where sediments have compacted. Beckles Willson refers to a firm, stony, gravelly surface, similar to that of the high country, being exposed by excavation. That does not sound as if it was originally in an area of sedimentation, so maybe Dugdale's opinion that an earthquake may have lowered the general level of a large tract of firm, dry land by several feet, is correct, and that the compaction of sedimentary areas was merely one of its more dramatic but additional effects. If the Wash area was part of the tract of land which was lowered several feet, that would have a favourable impact on the discussion of the practicality of a ford or ferry.

It is, as has been said, a geologically complex area, but nevertheless, perhaps we ought to try and form a picture in our minds of the pre-inundation Fenland of AD60 as boggy and marshy in places, intersected by many sluggish streams and rivers, and also consisting of areas forested with oak, pine, alder and nut trees.

If anyone is interested in a more practical confirmation of the Fen inundation, they might like to peruse a map of Roman roads and walk along one which goes south from Barton on the Humber, or one which goes east from Grantham, for both disappear into the rich, dark farmland a few miles from Boston.

Perhaps reading about this possibility of a catastrophic inundation of the Fen and Wash area in the 4th century has stimulated the same thoughts in your mind as came into my own. They are hypothetical and highly speculative, but logical to some degree, so they ought to be put into words before we move on.

At the point where rivers or their estuaries are crossed by roads, a settlement often comes into being, which may in time develop into a town. That, after all, was the way London came about. There are several names of Roman towns recorded in Britain, the sites of which have never yet been positively identified. One of those might be the name of the Iceni capital of AD43. Caistor-by-Norwich (Roman Venta) is rated by some for this accolade, but archaeology has failed to find convincing evidence that it was so. However, a site where the Icknield Way and Peddars Way perhaps crossed the Metaris estuary, with its access to a vast hinterland of navigable waterways, would also be a good contender. At such a place the collection of tolls from traders both on land and sea would have made the Iceni king a rich man, as we are told Prasutagus was, and such a place would not be far from Snettisham either, where the great hoard of gold torcs and other treasures was possibly buried in haste beneath a royal building, perhaps when the Iceni rebelled.

If the Iceni capital had been on the chalk ridge north of Hunstanton, then it obviously now lies beneath the waves, but there may also have been another small town to the west, on the projected line of the Roman road that runs east from Grantham towards Boston before disappearing under the fens – where perhaps it meets the road running south from Barton. After all, near that Roman smithy at the Skynbeck sluice, under sixteen feet of Lincolnshire silt, there must surely be the remains of a village or a villa, or else a smithy would not have existed where it was.

So in Britain there may be at least one, perhaps even more, nearly complete Romano–British towns, villages or villas of circa 300–400AD, preserved in the silt of the now drained Fens, much as Pompeii and Herculaneum were preserved by the volcanic material that issued from Vesuvius. That will be derided as fantasy and pure speculation – if there were to be nothing there other than the remains of that Roman smithy, but if the trowels of tomorrow's archaeologists were to find that there was, no doubt it will be considered an obvious deduction from genuine historical clues.

It is time now to finish setting the scene for AD43, by looking at the political situation in Britain, prior to the Roman invasion.

CHAPTER IV

The Political Situation
circa AD43

We now have some idea of what the countryside and climate of Britain might have been like circa AD43, and the way of life of some of its inhabitants, but we need to superimpose on that an internal political dimension, and then assess what relationships existed at that time with its nearest continental neighbour – Roman dominated Gaul.

Britain's society was tribal, and whatever their ancestral heritage, common or otherwise, those tribes clearly considered themselves to be culturally different from their neighbours. We need to know only a little about the psychology of modern football club supporters to form the opinion that there would have occasionally been friction between tribes, which would have led to raids, punch-ups or outright warfare. Tacitus confirmed that when he told us that the tribes generally fought amongst themselves on an annual basis. Obviously the strengths of those various tribes would have ebbed and flowed over a period of time, and the boundaries between them would have moved as a consequence. It is from Julius Caesar that we first learn the names of some of the British tribes and their leaders.

Caesar's principal opponents when he came to this island were the aggressive Catuvellauni tribe, which then occupied much of modern Hertfordshire, with its capital based at or near Wheathampstead. He also mentions the Trinovantes of Essex as being one of the strongest tribes in the south-east of Britain. Strong or not, those Trinovantes sought Caesar's help against their western neighbours, the Catuvellauni, and got it, and it is from this moment that the Fates started weaving Britain into a Roman future.

Caesar and his allies won the subsequent battle, and the defeated Catuvellauni, under their King Cassivelaunus, were forced to give, as part of the terms of their submission, an undertaking, effectively to Rome, not to further molest the Trinovantes.

Caesar and his army, however, soon withdrew from Britain, and after a generation or so, having in the meantime founded themselves a new capital at St Albans, the Catuvellauni, under a new king, Tasciovanus,

25

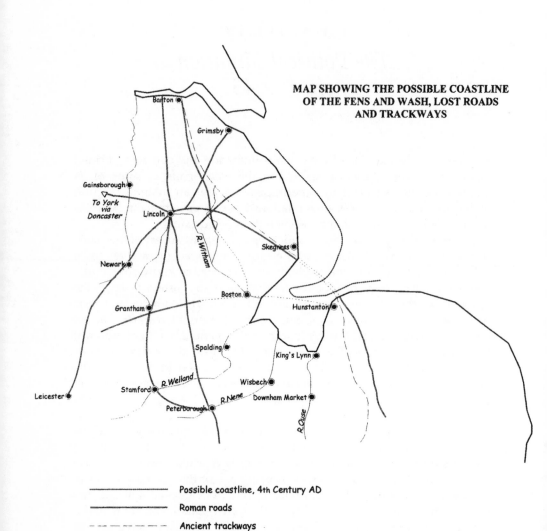

**MAP SHOWING THE POSSIBLE COASTLINE
OF THE FENS AND WASH, LOST ROADS
AND TRACKWAYS**

Barton

Grimsby

Gainsborough

To York
via
Doncaster

Lincoln

R. Witham

Skegness

Newark

Boston

Hunstanton

Grantham

Spalding

King's Lynn

Leicester

Stamford

R. Welland

Wisbech

Downham Market

Peterborough

R. Nene

R. Ouse

———————— Possible coastline, 4th Century AD

———————— Roman roads

– – – – – Ancient trackways

.... Projected routes of 'lost roads'

started to flex their muscles again, particularly against their old adversaries, the Trinovantes to the east. They must have been successful because by about AD10 the Trinovantes were under the total domination of the Catuvellauni, and as if to rub salt into their wounds, another new Catuvellauni capital was founded on or near the Trinovantes' old one at Colchester.

Precisely what influence Rome and the Emperor Augustus had, or thought they had, on the internal goings on in Britain at this time, is not clear. Some form of diplomatic protest may have been made, but if it was, it was ineffective. War with Britain was not in Augustus's mind, so, to all intents and purposes the Trinovantes' protector looked the other way and did nothing.

Cunobelin succeeded to the Catuvellauni kingship, and promptly proceeded to further expand his empire in other directions. Which could hardly have been encouraging news for the Atrebates tribe of Surrey and Sussex, which had earlier entered into an alliance of its own with Augustus.

Tiberius, when Augustus had passed on, also seems to have been content to let matters just drift along. Neither had curbed the Catuvellauni expansion, and consequently Cunobelin's empire gradually expanded still farther until it took in most of Kent and north Surrey, and also penetrated westward into the midlands. The neighbouring Iceni tribe of Norfolk may have been too strong and warlike for Cunobelin, for it appears to have been left alone.

For a time, Cunobelin's expansion plans went on hold – probably not because he was growing cautious or wiser, it was more likely that he was just growing older, and shortly after the death of Tiberius in AD37, Cunobelin divided his empire into three, and gave a part to each of his sons. One of these sons, Adminius, whose power base was the old capital Verulamium (St Albans), was pro-Roman, but the other two sons, Togodumnus and Caratacus, were implacably hostile to Rome. By the time Gaius had succeeded Tiberius as Emperor, the latter pair had attained sufficient control over their father to oust their brother Adminius, who then fled to Gaul. King Cunobelin of the Catuvellauni eventually died.

Togodumnus seems to have been the senior of the remaining two sons, for it was he who took over the larger part of the Catuvellauni empire, which was north of the Thames, leaving his brother Caratacus with that which was south of the river. Then both of them set about further expansion. The Cotswolds came under Togodumnus's influence, and Caratacus invaded the Atrebates territory of Surrey and Sussex. When his last remaining stronghold in southern Sussex fell, the Atrebates king, Verica, fled the country and went to Rome asking for help to restore him to his throne.

This time the situation was very different for Rome. The subjection of the Atrebates and the ousting of Verica had destroyed an essential buffer state, and left an actively hostile power facing the otherwise peaceful, and weakly garrisoned, north-west sea coast of Gaul. Possibly a few raiding parties had already crossed the channel to expose Gaul's vulnerability.

Four reasons are usually given for the invasion of Britain by Rome in AD43. The first is that the cost of keeping and provisioning extra troops along the coastline of Gaul, to counter raiding parties from the Catuvellauni, would probably have been greater in the long term than the expense incurred if those same troops were used to invade and subdue Britain – because when that goal had been successfully achieved, those troops could then subsist, free of charge, on Britain's agricultural produce and other resources.

Secondly, it was necessary, for Rome's honour and prestige, to be seen to go, even if a little belatedly, to the assistance of those to whom it was bound by treaty to protect and support – namely, Verica and the Atrebates tribe.

Thirdly, Claudius, who was now Emperor, wanted to achieve personal fame and honour by expanding the empire and having a great military victory won in his name. And fourthly, acquiring Britain's natural wealth, particularly its grain surplus and precious metals, had suddenly become an irresistible temptation.

Naturally any country considering the aggressive act of invading a neighbour will find as many reasons as possible to explain why such action is not only justifiable, but absolutely necessary, inevitable and unavoidable. Three of the above four reasons would undoubtedly have been put forward openly by the hawks in Rome. The other, about an easy Claudian prestige victory, was probably just an 'in' joke in the corridors of power, but it may have been the most important, in the mind of him whose opinion really mattered.

Anyway, Claudius made the decision that an invasion of Britain should take place, and orders to make that decision effective were subsequently issued.

CHAPTER V
The Roman Occupation
AD43 to AD47

In the summer of AD43 an army consisting of four legions, legios II, IX, XIV, and XX, together with an appropriate but unspecified number of auxiliaries and supporting troops, assembled on the coast of Gaul, probably at Boulogne, under the command of one Aulus Plautius, who had earlier been the governor of Pannonia, which was roughly today's Romania.

Tacitus's account of this period in his *Annals* has, unfortunately, been lost, so Dio Cassius must tell this part of Britain's history on his own.

> *Aulus Plautius, a senator of great renown, made a campaign against Britain; for a certain Bericus [Verica], who had been driven out of the island as the result of an uprising, had persuaded Claudius to send a force thither. Thus it came about that Plautius undertook this campaign; but he had difficulty in inducing his army to advance beyond Gaul. For the soldiers were indignant at the thought of carrying on a campaign outside the limits of the known world, and would not yield him obedience until Narcissus, who had been sent out by Claudius, mounted the tribunal of Plautius and attempted to address them.*

History has many facets, some deadly serious, some sublime, and others simply ridiculous. This event is one of the latter. The Roman invasion of Britain starts off as a complete farce. We are expected to believe that four tough, experienced Roman legions were so afraid of a short sea journey, which they must have known the great Caesar had once undertaken in two consecutive years, that they resorted to mutiny. That is hardly credible. This farce must have been contrived simply to give an ego inflation opportunity to one of Claudius's particular friend.

The story is so overtly childish that one wonders why Dio bothered to record it – but perhaps he had a dry sense of humour, because the farce did not work out as planned.

> *Then they [the soldiers] became much angrier at this and would not allow*

Narcissus to say a word, but suddenly shouted with one accord the well-known cry, 'Io Saturnalia' (for at the festival of Saturn the slaves don their master's dress and hold festival), and at once right willingly followed Plautius.

The very influential Narcissus was an ex-slave, so that cry of *'Io Saturnalia'* must, as was presumably intended, have been a humiliating insult. A single individual would probably not have got away with it, but who in their right mind would argue with four legions of angry, armed men? Those soldiers had most likely spent the past few weeks in intensive training and preparations for what could have been a hazardous sea-borne invasion, and they probably just wanted to get the landing over. Plautius must have had the patience of a saint, which is perhaps why he had been chosen to lead the campaign, for there was more farce and nonsense yet to come.

In the meantime, as a result of all the hanging about, there were, or might have been, problems.

Their delay, however, had made their departure late in the season.

That could have been dangerous. Caesar, a hundred years or so earlier, had been caught up in the English Channel's equinoctial gales, and nearly lost his fleet.

They were sent over in three divisions, in order that they should not be hindered in landing – as might happen to a single force – and in their voyage across they first became discouraged because they were driven back in their course, and then plucked up courage because a flash of light rising in the east shot across to the west, the direction in which they were sailing. So they put in to the island and found none to oppose them. For the Britons as a result of their inquiries, had not expected that they would come, and had therefore not assembled beforehand.

In 54BC Caesar needed 80 ships to convey his two legions to Britain, so Plautius's venture would probably have needed at least 160, which is quite a lot of shipping to be gathered in a small port on the fringes of the empire. Four full-strength legions would have consisted of about 24,000 troops, and the auxiliaries and cavalry might have numbered another 10,000 making 34,000 men in all. That works out at over 200 to each ship, plus all their horses, supplies and gear. One tends to think of all Roman ships as being stately triremes, or galleys of some sort, and indeed some probably were, but the majority were most likely requisitioned, local, Gaulish sail trading vessels, which would have been more suitable for bulk transport, and more seaworthy too.

Dio states that the Roman force was split into three divisions – so that they should not be hindered on landing – which suggests that there may have been three separate landing places. That might have been a risky ploy, for if the British had been able to concentrate their main force against only one of them, they might have overwhelmed it, and had Plautius lost a third of his strength on the first day, he might have turned tail and gone straight back to Gaul. As things turned out, though, it didn't matter – the British were not there in strength to oppose any landing.

Plautius may have used the delay caused by the Narcissus episode to his own advantage, as a ploy to fool the British into thinking that he was not going to invade after all, and that they did not need to mobilise. On the other hand, it is probably just as likely that the Britons had in fact assembled earlier, but had eaten all their rations, got fed up waiting, and dispersed.

It is often positively stated that the Romans landed at Richborough in Kent, but that is not necessarily correct. Dio does not name a specific place. In fact, Richborough is more nearly north of Boulogne, rather than west, which was the direction Dio says they sailed, so those landings may actually have taken place somewhere between Deal and Hastings, perhaps near Dover. It is quite possible, however, that the Emperor Claudius landed at Richborough on his later brief visit to Britain, and it would not be surprising if he were to have had a monument erected there to commemorate his so-called conquest of the island. That may have been the first of several impressive buildings constructed at Richborough. Anyway, Plautius, having safely landed somewhere, was having trouble finding someone to fight.

And even when they did assemble, they would not come to close quarters with the Romans, but took refuge in the swamps and the forests, hoping to wear out the invaders in fruitless effort, so that, just as in the days of Julius Caesar, they should sail back with nothing accomplished.

Plautius would not have wanted to advance far into hostile territory without subduing those areas he would be leaving behind him. So, having garrisoned a port – Dover possibly – to secure his shortest line of communication with Gaul, he probably sent out strong, wide-ranging patrols, before moving slowly and cautiously inland, searching for the elusive Britons.

Plautius, accordingly, had a deal of trouble in searching them out; but when at last he did find them, he first defeated Caratacus and then Togodumnus, the sons of Cynobellinus [Cunobelin], who was dead. (The Britons were not free and independent, but were divided into groups under various kings.) After the flight of these kings he gained by capitulation a part of the Dobunni, who were ruled by a tribe of the Catuvellauni; and leaving a garrison there, he advanced farther and came to a river.

That is one of the troubles with Dio, and with Tacitus too when he comes on stream. He gives us an unnecessary story about Narcissus at some length, then covers, in just a few lines, two important battles and a significant capitulation. The reason is probably that Rome had had so many battle victories that the writer's audiences would simply have been bored by accounts of yet more, unless they were exceptional in some way.

One can understand Caratacus making contact with the Romans first, since Kent was part of his territory, but it is surprising that he apparently did not wait to join forces with his brother before fighting a battle. It is, of course, possible that they were operating independently with the plan of creating a pincer movement to isolate and destroy a part of the Roman army. If that is what they intended, they obviously did not succeed – perhaps Plautius caught them napping with some smart manoeuvres of his own.

There is another possible reason why they may have fought separately. It would not be difficult to imagine that two characters such as they, who had already managed to topple one brother out of the Catuvellauni tribal nest, might then have set out to do the same thing again – to each other. Thus making an almost biblical scenario of the kind of brotherly love in which the winner takes all. Certainly nothing is heard of Caratacus again for several years, and then he turns up far away in Wales. He may have high-tailed it there straight from his battle with Plautius, leaving his brother, like Uriah the Hittite, to face the invaders, and possible annihilation, alone. On the other hand, to be fair, he may have fought bravely later on by the side of his beloved brother.

The initial British resistance was clearly ineffective – and the Dobunni tribe must have taken the first opportunity they were given to shake off the shackles of Caratacus's Catuvellauni, by submitting to the invaders. Perhaps they thought that the Romans could not possibly be worse task-masters than their fellow Britons, and they might have been right.

Anyway, Plautius had come to a river – the Medway, we must suppose. Dio continues:

> *The barbarians thought that the Romans would not be able to cross it without a bridge, and consequently bivouacked in a rather careless fashion on the opposite bank; but he* [Plautius] *sent across a detachment of Germans, who were accustomed to swim easily in full armour across the most turbulent streams.*

It is doubtful if anyone could swim easily in full armour, so possibly these German troops had adopted the Alexander the Great ploy of crossing rivers using inflated bladders or skins as buoyancy aids.

> *These fell unexpectedly upon the enemy, but instead of shooting at any of the*

men they confined themselves to wounding the horses that drew their chariots; and in the confusion that followed not even the enemy's mounted warriors could save themselves. Plautius thereupon sent across Flavius Vespasian also (the man who afterwards became emperor) and his brother Sabinus, who was acting as his lieutenant. So they, too, got across the river in some way and killed many of the foe, taking them by surprise.

This is no set piece battle and it all sounds rather scrappy. There is no excuse, of course, for the British allowing themselves be taken by surprise. The placing of sentries and picquets to warn of an approaching enemy is pretty basic stuff; and even a mere novice would be expecting the Roman troops to work their way up the banks of the river until it shallowed and was fordable. Even so, the Romans were not having the walk-over victory that Dio at first implies. In fact, it seems to have been a near run thing.

The survivors, however, did not take to flight, but on the next day joined issue with them again. The struggle was indecisive until Gnaeus Hosidius Geta, after narrowly missing being captured, finally managed to defeat the barbarians so soundly that he received the 'ornamenta triumphalia', though he had not been consul. Thence the Britons retired to the river Thames at a point near where it empties into the ocean and at flood-tide forms a lake. This they easily crossed because they knew where the firm ground and the easy passages in this region were to be found; but the Romans in attempting to follow them were not so successful. However the Germans swam across again and some others got over by a bridge a little way upstream, after which they assailed the barbarians from several sides at once and cut down many of them.

So the German swimmers were at it again, but that bridge a little way upstream may have been a floating pontoon bridge made from boats lashed together. The Roman navy, although Dio does not mention them, may possibly have been cruising along the north Kent coast, keeping pace with Plautius's advance.

The Romans had crossed the Thames, and were now established on the north bank in some numbers. Dio continues:

In pursuing the remainder incautiously, they got into swamps from which it was difficult to make their way out, and so lost a number of men. Shortly afterwards Togodumnus perished, but the Britons, so far from yielding, united all the more firmly to avenge his death.

So the Romans came to a terrified halt – as far as reports to the readers in Rome were concerned. Another imperial farce had to be played out. One feels a little sympathy for poor Aulus Plautius. Dio, with the party line:

Because of this fact and because of the difficulties he had encountered at the Thames, Plautius became afraid, and instead of advancing any farther, proceeded to guard what he had already won, and sent for Claudius. For he had been instructed to do this in case he met with any particularly stubborn resistance, and, in fact, extensive equipment, including elephants, had already been got together for the expedition.

Elephants, for heaven's sake. Whatever next?

Plautius was clearly under orders to halt at this point, so that Claudius could come with his 'extensive equipment', take over the command of the army, and fight a stage-managed battle which he could claim as his 'Victory triumph over the British'. One cannot help but wonder if the Catuvellauni resistance had, in fact, totally collapsed after Togodumnus's death, rather than intensified.

This was still AD43, apparently. Dio said that the invasion occurred later in the season than had been planned, and all Plautius's manoeuvres must have taken time too – so how near then was winter? Was Claudius, with his entourage and elephants, really going to face the autumnal gales that had nearly wrecked Julius Caesar's fleet?

While he waited for the Emperor, Plautius would not have been idle. There would have been areas south of the Thames yet to be subdued, a commissariat organisation to set up, storehouses to build, and forts to guard them. The road from Richborough or Dover would have needed improvement for when Claudius and his elephants arrived, and there would still have been some fighting to do.

The client king Verica of the Atrebates, who may have romanised his name to Claudius Tiberius Cogidumnus, needed to be reinstated to power in Sussex, to demonstrate that the Romans honoured their treaties. That task may have been given to the future emperor, Flavius Vespasian, who commanded the IInd legion, thanks to the influence of that ex-slave Narcissus.

Gaius Suetonius Tranquillus wrote a chapter on Vespasian's life in his *The Twelve Caesars*. This is his account of the future Emperor's time in Britain.

On Claudius' accession, Vespasian was indebted to Narcissus for the command of a legion in Germany; and proceeded to Britain, where he fought thirty battles, subjugated two warlike tribes, and captured more than twenty towns, besides the entire Isle of Vectis [the Isle of Wight]. In these campaigns he served at times under Aulus Plautius, the commander of consular rank, and at times directly under Claudius, earning triumphal decorations . . .

Vespasian was obviously a busy man. However, those achievements probably also include the battles in Kent, the Medway and the Thames, rightfully honours of Plautius. One of the war-like tribes that was subjugated may have been either the Belgae of Hampshire, or that part of the Catuvellauni which, under Caratacus, had conquered the Atrebates and ousted King Verica. The other war-like tribe is generally accepted as being the Durotriges of Devon and Dorset.

One would presume that Vespasian started his independent campaign by moving south from London to reinstate Verica, or Cogidumnus, at the Atrebates capital, which was probably not far from Chichester, perhaps at Fishbourne near Bosham harbour, where there are the remains of a magnificent palace.

To survive, even client kings need a secure base, and a solid organisational structure, with themselves firmly planted at the top. Perhaps, while that was being set up, Vespasian got his hands on some ships, and went to sort out the Isle of Wight. Then, back on the mainland he probably marched westward on the ancient chalk-ridge tracks, which were the only existing roads then, to deal with any further resistance, which he doesn't seem to have had any problem finding. The twenty towns he captured are assumed to have been inhabited hill forts. Some may have submitted meekly, but others only after hard fought battles. Graphic evidence of war, considered by archaeologists as being from this period, has come from excavations at the hill-forts of Maiden Castle and Hod Hill. At the former a direct assault had been mounted at the east gate before it had capitulated. At the latter it would appear that the chieftain's house had been bombarded with bolts and other missiles. Some of those thirty battles may have taken place after Claudius's visit, because Vespasian does seem to have returned to the area later.

While Vespasian was thus occupied, Aulus Plautius had probably been applying subtle threats and diplomatic pressures on the leaders of the various tribes, persuading them to voluntarily accept a Roman administration. He may also have insisted that they come to make a symbolic personal capitulation to Claudius in person, but only after a mock battle had been staged against the legions on the north bank of the Thames.

Those tribes probably included the Atrebates, Trinovantes, Dobunni, Catuvellauni, Iceni, Coritani, Belgae and the Cantii. That is a list of only eight, but a total of eleven tribal chiefs apparently appear submitting to Claudius on a commemoratory Roman frieze or carving, but who they actually were, or whether any of the tribes of the West Country or Wales were among them, is not known.

The Emperor Claudius was on his way. This is Dio's account of his journey.

When the message reached him, Claudius entrusted affairs at home, including the command of the troops, to his colleague Lucius Vitellius, whom he had caused to remain in office like himself for a whole half-year; and he himself then set out for the front. He sailed down the river to Ostia, and from there followed the coast to Massilia; thence, advancing partly by land and partly along the rivers, he came to the ocean and crossed over to Britain, where he joined the legions that were waiting for him near the Thames. Taking over the command of these, he crossed the stream, and engaged the barbarians, who had gathered at his approach, he defeated them in battle and captured Camulodunum [Colchester], the capital of Cynobellinus. Thereupon he won over numerous tribes, in some cases by capitulation, in others by force, and was saluted as 'imperator' several times, contrary to precedent, for no one man may receive this title more than once for one and the same war. He deprived the conquered of their arms and handed them over to Plautius, bidding him also subjugate the remaining districts. Claudius himself now hastened back to Rome . . . after an absence of six months, of which he had spent only sixteen days in Britain.

That is the official story, which excludes any further mention of the elephants, which might, of course, without the exhortations of Narcissus, have refused to board ship at Boulogne.

We are fortunate enough to have another, rather more cynical account of the Emperor's visit to Britain. Suetonius Tranquillus has this to say in his chapter on the life of Claudius in *The Twelve Caesars*:

Claudius' sole campaign was of no great importance. The Senate had already voted him triumphal regalia, but he thought it beneath his dignity to accept these, and decided that Britain was the country where a real triumph could be most readily earned. Its conquest had not been attempted since Julius Caesar's day; and the Britons were now threatening vengeance because the Senate refused to return certain deserters [Adminius and Verica?]. Sailing from Ostia, Claudius was twice nearly wrecked off the Ligurian coast, and again near the Stoechades Islands, but made port safely at Massilia. In consequence he marched north through Gaul until reaching Gesoriacum; crossed the channel from there; and was back in Rome six months later. He had fought no battles and suffered no casualties, but reduced a large part of the island to submission.

Suetonious suggests that Claudius's journey back took nearly six months, but that may not be correct. Dio said that he hastened, and one would certainly have thought that he would not have wanted to be away from the political intrigues of Rome for any longer than necessary.

His triumph [that is to say the festival held in Rome to celebrate his 'triumph'] was a very splendid one, and among those whom he invited to witness it were his provincial governors, and certain exiles as well. The emblems of his victory included the naval crown, representing the crossing and conquest, so to speak, of the ocean which he set on the palace gable beside the civic crown. His wife, Messalina, followed the chariot in a covered carriage, and behind her marched the generals who had won triumphal regalia in Britain. All wore purple-bordered togas except Marcus Crassus Frugi; having earned this same honour on a previous occasion, he now came dressed in a palm-embroidered tunic and rode a caparisoned charger.

That little section, 'behind her marched the generals who had won triumphal regalia in Britain', is interesting. If that included Plautius, Vespasian, Geta, Frugi and other senior officers, who on earth was left in charge of Britain while they were all away in Rome showing off their purple-bordered togas, or prancing about on caparisoned chargers? It would take whoever was there a month or so to travel all the way back to work. But they probably didn't hurry – it must have been winter in Britain by then, and the Roman troops could, no doubt, look after themselves. They would have made themselves comfortable in ditched wooden forts, and would have been content to spend the long evenings round the fire, yarning about women, or their exploits in half forgotten battles, while tippling the wine and trying out the strengths of locally brewed British real ales.

Aulus Plautius remained as governor of Britain until fairly late in AD47, but after Claudius's triumph celebrations Dio's references to this country become sparse and scrappy for a while. The lost sections of Tacitus's *Annals* might have helped us to piece together how the Romans set about organising the infrastructure of their newest province, but we must do what we can without them.

First though, the little snippets of other information that are available. Tacitus, in the *Agricola*:

Certain states were presented to King Cogidumnus, who maintained his unswerving loyalty down to our own times – an example of the long-established Roman custom of employing even kings to make others slaves.

The question here is which states? With Cogidumnus's base presumed to be near Chichester it would be reasonable to assume that one of them might be the adjacent tribe of the Hampshire Belgae. The Cantii may have been another – but so too may the Kent Dobunni. Maps showing tribal areas often lump all those southern tribes under the name of Regni, but that word merely means 'king's', so it is not a new clan that has suddenly appeared. Many authorities give Cogidumnus the whole of south-east England from Dorchester to London and Dover – which is quite a chunk of land. Cogidumnus must have been a good administrator and thoroughly romanised, or at least considered totally reliable. Incidentally, if Cogidumnus was, say, in his twenties in AD43, and was yet still alive fifty odd years later when Tacitus wrote his *Agricola*, he certainly lived to a ripe old age.

The next snippet is from Dio Cassius, circa AD47:

> *In Britain Vespasian had on a certain occasion been hemmed in by the barbarians and been in danger of destruction, but his son Titus, becoming alarmed for his father, managed by unusual daring to break through their enclosing lines and then pursued and destroyed the fleeing enemy.*

The translator of Dio makes the comment here that Vespasian's son, Titus, was born in the year AD39, so there is obviously something wrong with this piece of information; and that is compounded by the fact that Suetonius Tranquillus states that Titus was in fact born on 30 December AD41, so the incident is clearly reported erroneously. Perhaps Dio is mistakenly referring to a battle which occurred later in Vespasian's life, or alternatively that particular Titus was someone other than his son. If this quote does relate to Britain, then we may suppose that Vespasian had resumed his work in the West Country, sorting out the Durotriges and the Dumnonii tribes with his IInd legion, and things at some point in time had not gone quite according to plan.

To support the premise that Vespasian had strong connections with the West Country, there is a rather confused story in Geoffrey of Monmouth's 12th-century *History of the Kings of Britain*, in which Arvirargus (Caratacus?), who is the second son of Cymbeline (Cunobelin?), becomes King of Britain on the death of his brother Guierius (Togodumnus?), and then chases the Emperor Claudius all over the country. Eventually Vespasian turns up to besiege Exeter, but is himself then besieged by Caratacus.

It would be interesting to know Geoffrey's source for this story. He must certainly have found some ancient reference linking Vespasian or the IInd legion to Exeter, which is where we have deduced he may again have been active.

Aulus Plautius was replaced as governor in AD47. Dio:

> *Plautius for his skilful and successful conduct of the war in Britain not only was praised by Claudius but also obtained an ovation.*

It is nice to know that the loyal, patient Aulus Plautius got a pat on the back from Claudius, but don't be too pleased. Dio goes on to say this about Plautius's bloodthirsty ovation celebrations in Rome:

> *. . . in the gladiatorial combats many persons took part, not only of the foreign freedmen but also the British captives. He used up ever so many men in this part of the spectacle and took pride in the fact.*

So how, during the past four years, had Plautius organised his occupying forces, in order to leave a fair chunk of south-east Britain in a relatively peaceful state? To answer that question we must weigh up his options and make some assumptions based on common sense and whatever skimpy evidence archaeology has turned up.

We can make a start at Colchester or Camulodunum, the capital of the Catuvellauni, which Claudius had conquered in his probably stage-managed battles, because the Emperor seems to have decided to make that place the administrative capital of his new Roman province.

That is not a stated fact from our sources so far, but Tacitus will tell us later that in AD60 the province had only two cities, namely Verulamium and Camulodunum – Londinium was merely a town used by traders. Of the two cities Camulodunum appears to have been the more important, since we learn that until AD48 the XXth legion was based there, and that by AD60 it had a stone-built temple dedicated to Claudius himself, and other important public buildings. There are no such positive indications of prestigious development in the centre of Verulamium at that time.

It is difficult for us to look at a modern map of this country without being aware of the over-powering strategic dominance of London, and even more difficult to believe that it wasn't always so from the beginning of time. Instead of all roads leading to Rome or London, at this point in Britain's history, all the roads the Romans constructed would ultimately have led to Camulodunum.

One of Plautius's priorities would have been to set up an administration department in the capital to control Britain's economy. He would obviously have needed to levy or requisition provisions to feed his troops and those natives or slaves working full time on all his new building projects. So storage facilities would be needed in the appropriate places as well as an internal transport system to move produce to where it was needed. Where possible taxes in the form of cash would have had to be assessed and collected, and the mineral wealth of the province would need to be located, developed and exploited.

To do all that properly Plautius would have needed maps of important topographical features, and reliable estimates of population, agricultural production, and industrial output. We can be fairly certain that while he may have spent the late winter months of AD43–AD44 in Rome celebrating Claudius's dubious triumphs, his surveyors in Britain, and their assistants and escorts, would have been doing a lot of cross-country riding.

No doubt, in the spring of AD44, there began a frantic period of activity for the architects, civil engineers and administrators of the Roman army. It is one thing for a general to scribe lines or mark crosses on a map, but quite another to convert those into the reality of a quality road or a solid defensible fortress with its own water supply, sewage disposal system and living accommodation. The Roman soldier, we are told, was trained in all sorts of technical skills as well as that of fighting, so they probably needed little more than just being pointed in the right direction. They would have done some of the more skilled work themselves, but for the heavy, dirty work they would only have needed to supervise the unsold slaves captured in earlier battles, and the conscripted working parties from the local tribes.

Initially the Roman buildings would have been made of timber, so a vast number of trees would have had to be felled and cut into long planks or beams. Blacksmiths would have been busy turning out saws and axes, hinges, nails and other metalwork. Kilns would have been firing roofing tiles and drainage pipes. Chalk and sand would have been needed for mortar, and gravel and stone for the roads. There would certainly never have been enough British carts and wagons in AD44 to move the heavy stuff about, so more would have had to be built, and horses and oxen collected and trained to draw them. Then there would have been all the clerks, with their indents and requisition forms, trying to make sure that everything ended up in the right place at the right time.

If there really was peace in those early years, it may well have been because so many of the hot-headed and rebellious British natives were too worn out and exhausted by working long hours on all the building sites that had suddenly sprung up over southern Britain.

What about the military situation? Where would the frontiers of the new province have been? We can be pretty certain that the Roman legions would soon have advanced west and north until they came up against serious opposition, then the frontier line would probably have been determined by the nearest natural features of the landscape that could be defended easily, such as geological escarpments or large rivers like the Severn and Trent. The Romans have, in fact, left us clues to roughly where the frontier may have been. There is a major Roman road that is now called the Fosse Way, which ran, or runs still, diagonally across England – from Devon in the south, through the midlands, to Lincolnshire and the Humber in the north. That road must surely have been built so that the legions could support each other by facilitating the rapid transfer of troops to any major trouble spot anywhere along its length. The road would not have been the frontier, of course. That would have been a series of forts and outposts farther to the west or north, supported by strongly manned, suitably sited legionary base camps. Those base camps would themselves have needed a good direct road link with Camulodunum, where Plautius seems to have based the XXth legion, no doubt to keep order in the home counties and oversee all the prestigious developments that a capital needs in order to fulfil its function, but also as a strategic military reserve that could quickly be sent out to reinforce any of the other three legions, if the need arose.

Where were the other three legions stationed? We've assumed that after

Claudius's visit, Vespasian's IInd legion went back to the south-west to confront the Durotriges and the Dumnonii of Devon and Cornwall. That may be so, but archaeology suggests their main base might, in those early years, have been Gloucester, in Dobunni territory. That makes quite good sense really. It would have been of prime importance to stabilise that particular region quickly if Rome was really to make money out of Britain. The Mendip hills were lead and silver country, and archaeology has determined that its mines were producing for the Romans quite early on in the occupation. There was tin in Cornwall, of course, so detachments of the IInd were probably sent there too.

A Roman road, which is now named Akeman Street, goes from Gloucester via Cirencester to Verulamium, and a road from there goes directly to Camulodunum. Perhaps Vespasian and the IInd legion built that or those, as a communications trunk road from the capital to their legionary base camp.

It is generally accepted that the XIVth legion was based at Wroxeter in the West Midlands, but that place is quite some distance north-west of the Fosse Way support road, and so as a base camp, on the map it does not look quite right. However, no other alternative seems ever to have been suggested. Wroxeter is on what is now called Watling Street, which appears to go straight to and from the river ford at Londinium, and just to confuse matters, it is also the name given to the road from London to Dover. However, near Leicester Watling Street joins up with another road called the Via Devana, which goes to Camulodunum through Huntingdon, Godmanchester and Cambridge. That is an almost straight line linking Wroxeter with Camulodunum, and it is a substantial road too, with an *agger* that is sometimes 33ft wide. So that might well have been the one the XIVth legion constructed. Watling Street south of Leicester may have been built later, or it could originally have been a pre-Roman track linking Togodumnus's part of the Catuvellauni empire with Caratacus's part south of the Thames.

Neither of those is particularly controversial, but the site of the IXth legion's headquarters camp, and its road to Camulodunum, may be. Some people favour a site near Peterborough, but that is quite some distance from the Fosse Way, and it would surely have been too far from its outposts on the Trent to adequately support them. Most authorities, however, believe that the IXth was based at Lincoln, even if archaeology cannot pin the legion there with certainty until after AD60. Lincoln, however, is on Ermine Street, which is better known as the A1, or the 'Great North Road'. It links London with Peterborough, Lincoln, York and all important places north to Edinburgh and beyond, but in AD43 some of those places may never have existed, and so it should not, as far as our basic premise will allow, relate to this period when Camulodunum was the capital. We are ideally looking for a direct road link from there to

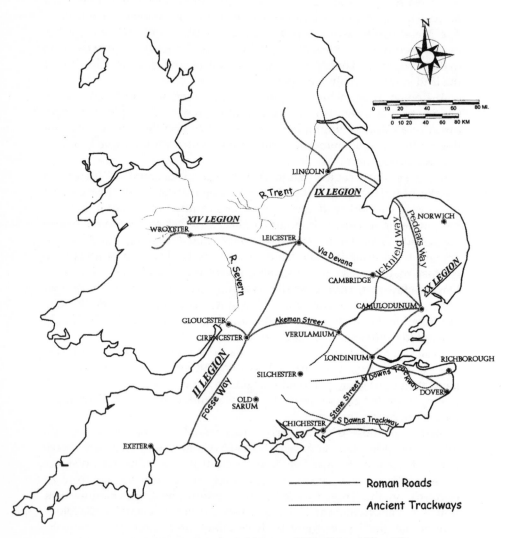

ROMAN BRITAIN CIRCA AD 47

Lincoln, and the only Roman road that will give us that is Peddars Way, which we have discussed at some length on earlier pages in connection with the proposition that the Wash was fordable or relatively easily crossed in AD43.

So, after four years of occupation the limits of British territory then subdued and settled would appear to have been defined by a rough line drawn a few miles to the west or north of the Fosse Way.

Perhaps the Roman authorities would have been happy to leave it there, if they could have done so without too much hassle from the tribes on the other side of the frontier. It would have given them most of what they might have considered valuable or economically worthwhile in the province. However, those frontier tribes were apparently not interested in peace, at least not on Roman terms. The IInd legion faced Devon, Cornwall and South Wales – the homelands of the Durotriges, Dobunni and Silures. The XIVth fronted central and North Wales and southern Cheshire, with its Cornovii and Ordovices tribes, while the IXth watched over Derbyshire, and the eastern Pennines to the Humber – home to the Brigantes and Parisi.

Some 18,000 Roman front-line troops, plus auxiliaries, were therefore guarding a frontier which was nigh on 260 miles long. For an era without the use of barbed wire and land mines it was a frontier which was thinly manned, and could obviously be pierced almost anywhere by determined bands of hill tribesmen, who, as they always seem to be in history, were fit, agile and extremely aggressive folk, envious of the richness of the more fertile lowlands, and not averse to helping themselves to some of its wealth, from time to time.

That has defined the frontier regions reasonably logically and placed the three legions responsible for guarding it, but the rest of southern Britain was not left under the sole control of the XXth legion based at Camulodunum. We now need to consider the part the two client kings played in Plautius's occupation plans.

Vespasian may have helped Cogidumnus get a firm grip of his territories in south-east England, and the commander of the IXth legion may have assisted the King of the Iceni, Prasutagus, to make any changes to his organisational and administrative structure necessitated by the new circumstances. The latter should not have been an onerous task, because unlike Cogidumnus, who had to be reinstated, as far as we know Prasutagus was a well established ruler. Nevertheless, no doubt the Romans advised him and checked everything out thoroughly, including, if he was allowed them, and we ought to presume that he was, his internal peace-keeping and law enforcement officers, and his revenue collectors.

As might be expected, in the lands of the Iceni and the Regni, which the Romans obviously considered peaceful and under control, there are few identified sites of forts, and there are none at all in south-east Lincolnshire.

So it may be that Prasutagus was also given control over some of the territory of a neighbouring tribe – in this case the Coritani. It would have made good administrative sense from the Roman point of view, but there is no written hint to suggest that it was so.

Presumably, with few of their troops needing to be stationed in the areas of those client kingdoms, there would have been no need for large Roman stores or granaries either. Any agricultural produce levied, particularly wheat, because the Romans liked their bread, would have best been transported directly to where it was needed during the still good weather immediately after harvesting.

To put things into perspective, between them King Cogidumnus and King Prasutagus were probably responsible for collecting revenues or tithes, and maintaining law and order, in quite a large proportion of the whole province, perhaps as much as a third of its total area. So those two individuals were very important people in the administrative set up of Roman Britain.

No other similar client kings are alluded to, although later on there appears to have been an undefined special relationship of a different kind between the Romans and Cartimandua, Queen of the Brigantes. In the rest of occupied Britain, where perhaps the upper levels of the traditional tribal control structure had been destroyed, or were considered unreliable, it is likely that the lesser tribal chiefs, or the headmen of smaller communities or villages, would have been delegated or co-opted into taking some kind of administrative responsibility in their local areas, but under the much closer supervision of Roman regional commissioners. No doubt the Roman authorities would have wanted to control all the civil population within the province without diverting any more of their forces than were absolutely necessary from the essential task of guarding the frontiers against the incursions of rebel tribesmen.

Plautius would probably have tried to get acceptance of Roman rule, or at least an agreed form of neutrality, from all those rebellious tribes on his frontier, either by diplomacy or bribery, before resorting to force, but if he did, he was not successful. Perhaps those hill tribes had such a long tradition of raiding the richer lowlands that they would have disputed the authority of anyone who tried to deny them that freedom of action, including their own nominal leadership.

We have only mentioned briefly an important part of the Roman infra-structure – their roads – which are famed for their durability. They were probably built so well in order to minimise the need for subsequent maintenance, which is good economics. They did not always follow the line of the shortest distance between two points, but they were made as straight as they could reasonably be. The better the visibility ahead the less risk of an ambush, but it wasn't just that on a straight, even surface troops marching in a military emergency could travel faster and farther in a set period of time; so too, in times of peace, could the messenger, the general traveller, and just as importantly, the wagons of a supply convoy. An efficient transport system meant that fewer wagons and oxen were needed than would otherwise be the case; which also makes good sense.

For a technical description of the construction of their roads we can do no better than refer to the instructions written down by a famous engineer of the time named Vitruvius.

> *A road should be made up of four layers of different materials, the bottom one of beaten earth, the second of small stone lumps made rigid by the pouring in of mortar, the third of gravel or pounded tiles and sand, and the top layer either set with paving-stones or with a firm bed of gravel well rammed down.*

The Romans gave the name *agger* to the embankment thus raised, and its width would vary, depending on the road's strategic purpose or rating, from 18 feet or less for the minor roads, to as much as 30 feet or more for the major roads. It would be ditched on both sides to ensure good drainage, and all the trees and undergrowth would be cleared away from either side, for at least as far as would ensure that there was no fear of marching troops being unexpectedly attacked or ambushed.

We may presume that Aulus Plautius, Britain's first Roman Governor had organised the affairs of the new province in a suitably sound military and business-like manner. Claudius, we know, thought so.

So, in AD47 Plautius went back to Rome, to enjoy his 'ovation' by organising the slaughter of all those poor British captives in gladiatorial combat. His successor as governor was Ostorius Scapula.

CHAPTER VI

Britain AD48 to AD60

We are now through the period covered by the lost section of Tacitus's *The Annals of Imperial Rome,* so he can take up the story.

According to Aulus Plautius and the Emperor Claudius, the new Roman province of Britain was now a peaceful place. Someone was not telling the truth. In the *Annals,* Tacitus wrote:

> *In Britain the situation inherited by the imperial governor, Publius Ostorius Scapula, was chaotic. Convinced that a new commander, with an unfamiliar army and with winter begun, would not fight them, hostile tribes had broken violently into the Roman province. But Ostorius knew that initial results are what produce alarm or confidence. So he marched his light auxiliary battalions rapidly ahead, and stamped out resistance. The enemy were dispersed and hard pressed.*

It is unlikely that a change of governor, even if the British grapevine or news service was capable of passing such information on to the lower echelons of native society, would have bothered the hostile tribes one little bit. What is more likely is that the legions on the frontier were seriously getting in the way of the traditional tribal annual raiding parties.

Ostorius was obviously out to demonstrate that he was the big white chief in Britain and would stand no nonsense. Perhaps that was why he then went on to do something which would inevitably stir up more trouble. Tacitus continues:

> *To prevent a rally, or a bitter treacherous peace which would give neither general or army any rest, Ostorius prepared to disarm all suspects and reduce the whole territory as far as the Trent and Severn.*

Tacitus clearly said that the troublesome tribes came *into* the Roman province. For Ostorius to think he could solve that problem by disarming and thus humiliating those British who had so far been co-operating with the Romans, or at least not causing any great trouble, does not make a great deal of sense. One rather gets the feeling that Ostorius tended to go at things like a bull at a gate. Anyway, the result of what he did was inevitable.

> *The first to revolt against this were the Iceni. We had not defeated this powerful tribe in battle, since they had voluntarily become our allies. Led by them, the neighbouring tribes now chose a battlefield at a place protected by a rustic earthwork, with an approach too narrow to give access to cavalry. The Roman commander, though his troops were auxiliaries without regular support, proposed to carry these defences. At the signal, Ostorius' infantry, placed at appropriate points and reinforced by dismounted cavalrymen, broke through the embankment. The enemy, imprisoned by their own barrier, were overwhelmed – though with rebellion on their consciences, and no way out, they performed prodigies of valour. During the battle the governor's son, Marcus Ostorius Scapula, won the Citizen's Oak-Wreath for the saving of a Roman's life.*

The Iceni's neighbouring tribes could have been the Coritani, the Catuvellauni, or the Trinovantes. The battle site does not sound like an Iron Age ring fort, as is suggested by some historians, who favour one near Holkham in Norfolk. Tacitus's description rather suggests a valley with a hastily erected earthwork barricade across its entrance. Ostorius still had no regular troops with him, only his auxiliary infantry – and dismounted cavalrymen. If those dismounted cavalrymen were some of Prasutagus's mobile police force, it might explain why that king seems to have got away with his failure to control his rebellious subjects on that occasion.

The rebels performed prodigies of valour? That is something barbarians are usually only allowed to do in Roman accounts when an audience needs to be impressed for some reason. Marcus Ostorius Scapula, the governor's son, won a Citizen's Oak-Wreath for bravery – that might explain it.

> *This defeat of the Iceni quieted others who were wavering between war and peace.*
> *The Roman army then struck against the Decangli, ravaging their territory and collecting extensive booty.*

The Decangli were a North Wales tribe in the Flint–Bangor area. This time, presumably, Ostorius had troops from the XIVth legion with him, and possibly the prospect of 'extensive booty' may have been an encouragement for them to leave their comfortable winter quarters for a while.

> *The enemy did not venture upon an open engagement and, when they tried to ambush the column, suffered for their trickery.*

Ostorius had nearly reached the sea facing Ireland when a rising by the Brigantes recalled him. For, until his conquests were secured, he was determined to postpone further expansion. The Brigantes subsided; their few peace-breakers were killed, and the rest were pardoned. But neither sternness nor leniency prevented the Silures [from South Wales] from fighting. To suppress them, a brigade garrison had to be established. In order to facilitate the displacement of troops westward to man it, a strong settlement of ex-soldiers was established on conquered land at Camulodunum. Its mission was to protect the country against revolt and familiarise the provincials with law-abiding government. Next Ostorius invaded Silurian territory.

Ostorius obviously needed extra troops out on the South Wales frontier, but it would seem that the Emperor wasn't prepared to give him any more than he had already been allocated.

The XXth legion, based at Camulodunum, presumably had little to do at that time but hang about waiting for the emergency which might send them scurrying along one of those arterial roads to reinforce the front line. However, Ostorius could not move them permanently without making some other plans to ensure the security of the city and the eastern home counties. So he set up a *colonia* there.

Which means that soldiers retiring from active service, instead of returning to their original homes, would be offered grants of land, which were presumably large enough for them to become gentlemen farmers, in the countryside near to the *colonia* or city. In return for this generous and attractive bounty, they would form a Dads' Army – a military reserve which could be called upon to defend the city in an emergency, whilst at the same time setting an example of good citizenship to the local natives, and presumably siring a whole string of future legionaries.

To make this new *colonia* at Camulodunum immediately effective, Ostorius would have needed to instantly retire a significant number of veteran troops, and at the same time bring in an equally large number of recruits to replace them.

When it was initially raised, or when it was replacing heavy battle casualties, a legion may have taken in a high proportion of young recruits who, at a later date, would all reach retirement age at much the same time – so it would not be impossible for the XXth to already have become a collection of near time-served grey-beards. Indeed that may be the reason why it was given duties in the Home Counties rather than being put into the more active front line.

Legions were recruited from different parts of the vast empire, and although they were all technically Roman citizens, there must inevitably have been language and cultural differences between them. We are not told whether these newly retired ex-soldiers came from each of the four legions, or only from the XXth. It would be interesting to know for certain, because there is a passage in Tacitus's *Annals* about the problems of new *colonias* being set up with troops from different legions. It is nearly contemporary with the setting up of the Camulodunum settlement, but is not about Britain. It may be relevant though.

> *In the same year, in Italy, the ancient town of Puteoli was given the status of a Roman settlement and named after Nero. The settlements at Tarentum and Antium, too, were augmented by ex-soldiers. But this did not arrest their depopulation. For most of the settlers emigrated to the provinces in which they had served – leaving no children, since they were unaccustomed to marrying and bringing up families. Once these settlements had consisted of whole brigades of soldiers drawn up in their ranks behind their officers – a new community based on consent and comradeship. But now colonists came from various units and were unknown to each other. Without leaders, without loyalty, they were a mere concentration of aliens rather than a Roman settlement.*

Clearly a *colonia* made up of veterans from more than one unit did not always achieve the desired objective.

The whole of the XXth legion would not have been stationed at Camulodunum, of course. Probably more than half would have been detached to form the garrisons of various storage depots, forts or outposts, even those as far away as Dover. If Ostorius had wanted to move a complete legion to the front line, he would also have had to find replacements for those from his auxiliaries, or have reduced the garrison sizes.

The colony was to be a 'strong' settlement, but how many troops are 'strong'? A thousand, or a few hundred, must surely be too weak to be able to defend a provincial city, so perhaps it was nearer two thousand initially.

The length of service for a legionary in the Roman army was then apparently sixteen years. Therefore, an average of some 400 would have been discharged annually from a legion of 6,000 troops. After twelve years, which would take us up to AD60, the year of Queen Boudicca's rebellion, there may have been as many as 4,500 additional settlers to add to the initial contingent, but that total would need adjusting to allow for subsequent deaths and because some veterans may not have taken up the land allocation. So if we cautiously halve our figures, we end up with a very rough estimate of there perhaps being between 2,500 and 3,500 retired legionaries actually in the colony by AD60. Which at least sounds as if it were a strong enough force to defend the city in an emergency.

If each grant of land had originally supported a native family unit of say six, then there could have been as many as 21,000 displaced or distressed Trinovantes. Which is quite a lot of people. According to Tacitus it was conquered land, so there would have been no compulsory purchase compensation schemes. Would the natives have been ejected from their homes and left to starve? It is far more likely that they were forced to stay, and become the slaves of the newcomers.

Anyway, back to AD48. With their numbers presumably brought up to strength by an influx of new recruits, the XXth legion set off to take over the Gloucester section of the front line from the IInd legion, who then appear to have moved down to Exeter. Perhaps, in hindsight, Ostorius would have been wiser to have sent the XXth legion to Exeter, and left the more battle-wise IInd legion to face one of the most troublesome and aggressive of all the tribes – the Silures of South Wales. On the other hand, perhaps the tribes in Devon and tin-rich Cornwall also needed to be confronted by a strong force.

Now we meet up again with Caratacus, whom we last heard of back in AD43, shortly before Aulus Plautius's battle of the Medway. Unknown to us, he had, apparently, been making quite a name for himself. Tacitus writes in the *Annals* (c. AD50):

> *The natural ferocity of the inhabitants was intensified by their belief in the prowess of Caratacus, whose many undefeated battles – and even many victories – had made him pre-eminent among British chieftains. His deficiency in strength was compensated by superior cunning and topographical knowledge.*

How on earth did Caratacus end up in South Wales.? One tends to think of the Silures as a tough bunch of suspicious, brigand-like characters, as ready to cut the throat of a stranger as blink an eye, and it is difficult to imagine them welcoming with open arms a foreigner who suddenly turns up with a family and large entourage, all of whom would need accommodation and feeding. Perhaps that supposedly powerful Druid organisation brokered a safe haven for him with the local Silurian chiefs, or he may have been related to them in some way, possibly through the female line. Of course, if he'd fetched enough Catuvellauni treasure away with him, he might have bought his way into Silurian favour. Any of those suggestions would be understandable if his intentions were merely to retire peacefully into the background, but for him to use their lands as a terrorist base, from which to raid a mean and vicious enemy, who would inevitably retaliate in force, seems another thing entirely. So we may be wrong in assuming Caratacus had settled in South Wales just because he now turns up there. Tacitus awards him undefeated battles, and even victories, but his activities do not seem to have troubled Aulus Plautius much, or warranted a comment earlier from Dio.

That he may not have had the full support of the local tribes is suggested by 'His deficiency in strength'. So his force, although troublesome, may only have been a small raiding party. In which case perhaps we ought to consider the possibility that Caratacus had become a resistance or guerrilla leader based somewhere else, possibly in Anglesey, the Isle of Man, or even Ireland, who trained bands of rebels and sent them raiding against the Romans, perhaps occasionally leading one himself. All their victories might then have been told as his own, and it would explain Caratacus's immediate reaction to the Romans' attack on the Silurians.

> *Transferring the war to the country of the Ordovices* [middle to North Wales], *he was joined by everyone who found the prospect of a Roman peace alarming.*

So, once he'd stirred up a hornet's nest, Caratacus was quite happy to desert the Silurians, and leave them to suffer the wrath and vengeance of Rome, while he moved to another tribe's area. There he was probably joined by a whole load of fanatics, hot-heads and troublemakers, or perhaps they were all true patriots – but in enough numbers presumably to have made Caratacus rash and over confident. He may have done well with cunning, raids and ambushes, and he should have stuck to what he knew best.

> *Then Caratacus staked his fate on a battle. He selected a site where numerous factors – notably approaches and escape-routes – helped him and impeded us. On one side there were steep hills. Wherever the gradient was gentler, stones were piled into a kind of rampart. And at his front there was a river without easy crossings. The defences were strongly manned.*

Tacitus usually fails to give us any real detail in his accounts of battles. Well, there's plenty here, and more to come. The bit about the Welsh tribes defeating Julius Caesar, who never got anywhere near them, is amusing, and a little worrying, because Tacitus should have known that, if he'd done his homework properly.

> *The British chieftains went round their men, encouraging and heartening them to be unafraid and optimistic, and offering other stimulants to battle* [Welsh whisky? Cannabis?]. *Caratacus, as he hastened to one point and another stressed that this was the day, this the battle, which would either win back their freedom or enslave them for ever. He invoked their ancestors, who by routing Julius Caesar had valorously preserved their present descendants from Roman officials and taxes – and their wives and children from defilement. These exhortations were applauded. Then every man swore by his tribal oath that no enemy weapons would make them yield – and no wounds either.*
> *This eagerness dismayed the Roman commander, disconcerted as he*

1. The Emperor Claudius was the man who gave orders for the Roman invasion of Britain in AD 43. This is a replica of the head of Claudius from a large bronze statue erected at Colchester. The original is in the British Museum.
Photograph by the author – courtesy of Colchester Museum.

2. A model of the Temple erected at Colchester, in honour of the Emperor Claudius. The original must have taken a great deal of time and money to build, but it would not have looked as pristine as this when the British rebels had finished with it in AD 60.
Photograph by J Smallwood – courtesy of Colchester Museum.

3. All that remains of Claudius's Temple now are these vaults beneath Colchester Castle. Photograph by J Smallwood – courtesy of Colchester Museum.

4. The XXth legion were stationed at Colchester. The inscription on this tombstone reads: 'Marcus Favonius Facilis, Son of Marcus of the Pollian Voting Tribe, centurian of the Twentieth legion lies buried here; Verecundus and Novicius, his freedmen, set this up.' Photograph by J Smallwood – courtesy of Colchester Museum.

5. Another tombstone from Colchester. This is of a Cavalry officer who died a long way from his birthplace. The inscription reads: 'Longinus Sdapexe, son of Matygus Duplicarius from the First Cavalry Regiment of Thracians, from the district of Sardia, aged 40, of 15 years service, lies buried here; his heirs under his will had this set up.' Photograph by the author – courtesy of Colchester Museum.

6. Timber, mud, thatch and rope were the building materials of the British in AD 43, and, no doubt, for many generations before and since. Homes similar to the above, grouped into stockaded villages, as in plate 7 below, would have been replicated all over Britain. Roman building methods using mortar, brick, stone and tile, must have created something of a cultural shock even for the more sophisticated British.
Photograph by the author – courtesy of The Iceni Village, Cockley Cley, Swaffham, Norfolk.

7. A reconstruction of a British village circa AD 43.
Photograph by courtesy of The Iceni Village, Cockley Cley, Swaffham, Norfolk.

8. The Via Devana
Photograph by J Smallwood.

9. Peddars Way, Norfolk. Photograph by the author.

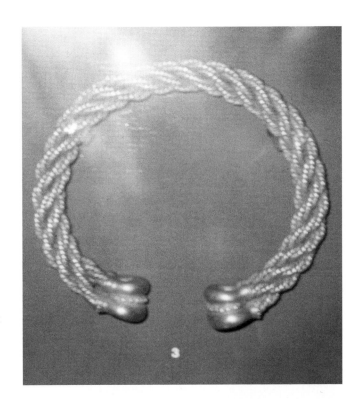

10. Gold Torc, found at Snettisham, Norfolk. Photograph by the author – courtesy of Norwich Museum.

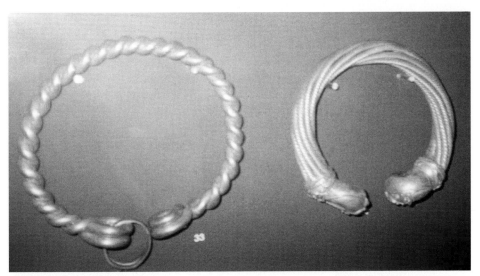

11. These are more Torcs from the Snettisham Treasure. In fact the whole collection is well worth seeing. Snettisham must have been an important place in the late Iron Age and more items of jewellery still turn up there occasionally. These, or similar such items, may have been in the wealthy King Prasutagus's strong boxes and thus been available to Queen Boudicca. The gold necklace Dio Cassius refers to in his description of her was probably a torc, which was a Celtic symbol of high status. Not necessarily a very comfortable thing to wear for any length of time as the ones of the highest quality are quite heavy, weighing several kilograms. Photograph by the author – courtesy of Norwich Museum.

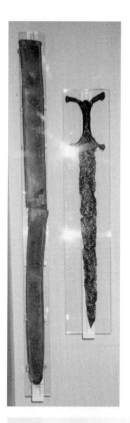

12. (left) A Celtic sword and a Bronze scabbard, both found in Norfolk. Photograph by the author – courtesy of Norwich Museum.

13. (right) The Witham Celtic shield. Possibly only for ceremonial purposes. Photograph by the author – courtesy of Lincoln and County Museum.

14. (left) This model shows a Legionary soldier in full armour.
Photograph by the author – courtesy of Lincoln and County Museum.

15. (right) A Tombstone from Wroxeter. The inscription reads: 'Marcus Petronius, son of Lucius, from the Menenian Voting Tribe, from Vicetia; aged 38, soldier with the XIVth Gemina Legion, with 18 years service. He was a standard bearer. He lies here'.
Photograph by P Ovington – courtesy of Shrewsbury Museum's Service.

16. Part of another Wroxeter Tombstone. The missing upper section would have been an impressive full length figure, but only the feet remain. The inscription is surprisingly moralistic, and reads: 'Titus Flaminus, Son of Titus, of the Pollian Voting Tribe, from Faventia, aged 45 with 22 years service. A soldier of the XIVth Gemina Legion. I did my service and now I am here. Read this and be either more or less fortunate in your life-time. The Gods prohibit you from the wine grape and water when you enter Tartarus. Live honourably while your star grants you time for life.'

Photograph by P Ovington – courtesy of Shrewsbury Museum's Service.

17. A Roman helmet. Photograph by the author – courtesy of Colchester Museum.

18. The IXth Legion was certainly based in Lincoln at some time in the early years of the Roman occupation. This tile, found in Lincoln, is impressed with the Legion's mark. Photograph by the author – courtesy of Lincoln and County Museum.

already was by the river barrier, the fortifications supplementing it, the overhanging cliffs, and the ferocious crowds of defenders at every point. But our soldiers shouted for battle, clamouring that courage could overcome everything; and their colonels spoke to the same effect, to encourage them further.

After a reconnaissance to detect vulnerable and invulnerable points, Ostorius led his enthusiastic soldiers forward. They crossed the river without difficulty, and reached the rampart. But then, in an exchange of missiles, they came off worse in wounds and casualties. However, under a roof of locked shields, the Romans demolished the crude and clumsy stone embankment, and in the subsequent fight at close quarters the natives were driven to the hill tops. Our troops pursued them closely. While light-armed auxiliaries attacked with javelins, the heavy regular infantry advanced in close formation. The British, unprotected by breastplates or helmets, were thrown into disorder. If they stood up to the auxiliaries they were cut down by the swords and spears of the regulars, and if they faced the latter they succumbed to the auxiliaries' broadswords and pikes. It was a great victory.

Caratacus' wife and daughter were captured; his brother surrendered. He himself sought sanctuary with Cartimandua, queen of the Brigantes. But the defeated have no refuge. He was arrested, and handed over to the conquerors.

With the number of 'ours' and 'theys', and the detail, it rather seems as though Tacitus may have lifted this account of the battle straight from some eye-witness's memoirs, but if he did, he makes no acknowledgement of doing so. Agricola was only 11 years old in AD50, so it cannot have come from him.

We have mentioned the possibility of Queen Cartimandua being a 'client queen', but her relationship with the Romans at that time may simply have been one of agreed neutrality. Giving Caratacus a refuge might have risked her tribe's well-being for no material benefit whatever. So, on the face of it, what she did is understandable. However, there might be a lot more behind this whole story than meets the eye, and it deserves a little more thought.

If Caratacus was leading a commando-style raiding party, why did he take his wife and daughter along with him? Another thing – the tribal area of the Brigantes was Cheshire, Lancashire, Derbyshire and Yorkshire – with Cartimandua's capital possibly being near York. Why, with Druid rich Anglesey and all the North Wales mountains close by to seek refuge in, should Caratacus have ended up in Brigantes territory, miles away from the battle site in the Ordovices' lands?

It is possible that he had made such a nuisance of himself that all Wales, other than those patriotic hot-heads, had turned against him, forcing him to travel a long way to seek what he ought to have known would be an unlikely haven with Cartimandua.

The readiness of Roman history to slip into farce makes one suspicious of this story. So perhaps Caratacus had become tired of being always on the run, and sought, through Cartimandua's good offices, a way of surrendering to the Romans which would save his life and the lives of his family. In other words, he may have cooked up a deal with Ostorius which involved a typical Roman spin doctor publicity stunt. By boosting Caratacus's anti-Roman achievements, Ostorius may have been able to present his capture or surrender as a *Victory* worthy of one of Rome's triumphal celebrations.

Is that unlikely? Perhaps – but Tacitus now gives us some really serious hype. Caratacus was not just a British celebrity – he has become a major international star player. With those thoughts in mind, read on and see what you think. In the *Annals*, Tacitus continues:

> *The war in Britain was in its ninth year. The reputation of Caratacus had spread beyond the islands and through neighbouring provinces to Italy itself. These people were curious to see the man who had defied our power for so many years. Even at Rome his name meant something. Besides, the emperor's attempts to glorify himself conferred additional glory on Caratacus in defeat.*

That last sentence is a strange one. Is Tacitus telling us *sotto voce* that it was all a con trick, arranged with Claudius's prior approval? Caratacus had, by now, been taken to Rome. From the *Annals* still:

> *For the people were summoned as though for a fine spectacle, while the Guard stood in arms on the parade ground before their camp. Then there was a march past, with Caratacus' petty vassals, and the decorations and neck-chains and spoils of his foreign wars. Next were displayed his brothers, wife and daughter. Last came the king himself. The others, frightened, degraded themselves by entreaties. But there were no downcast looks or appeals for mercy from Caratacus. On reaching the dais he spoke in these terms.*
>
> *'Had my lineage and rank been accompanied by only moderate success, I should have come to this city as friend rather than prisoner, and you would not have disdained to ally yourself peacefully with one so nobly born, the ruler of so many nations. As it is, humiliation is my lot, glory yours. I had horses, men, arms, wealth. Are you surprised I am sorry to lose them? If you want to rule the world, does it follow that everyone else welcomes enslavement? If I had surrendered without a blow before being brought before you, neither my downfall nor your triumph would have become famous. If you execute me, they will be forgotten. Spare me, and I shall be an everlasting token of your mercy!'*

That is quite an impressive speech, but it is probably Tacitus's rhetorical skills rather than Caratacus's silver tongue. It is perhaps unlikely that Caratacus was fluent enough in Latin or Greek to deliver any such speech, but whatever it was that he did say, it presumably had the desired, perhaps pre-planned, effect.

> *Claudius responded by pardoning him and his wife and brothers. Released from their chains, they offered to Agrippina, conspicuously seated on another dais nearby, the same homage and gratitude as they had given the emperor. That a woman should sit before Roman standards was an unprecedented novelty. She was asserting her partnership in the empire her ancestors had won.*
>
> *Then the senate met. It devoted numerous complimentary speeches to the capture of Caratacus. This was hailed as equal in glory to any previous Roman general's exhibition of a captured king. They cited the display of Syphax by Publius Cornelius Scipio Africanus and of Perseus by Lucius Aemilius Paullus. Ostorius received an honorary Triumph.*

Dio also comes up with his own interesting anecdote on this same event. So it must certainly have been a big thing in Rome.

> *Caratacus, a barbarian chieftain who was captured and brought to Rome and later pardoned by Claudius, wandered about the city after his liberation; and after beholding its splendour and its magnitude he exclaimed: 'And can you, then, who have got such possessions and so many of them, covet our poor tents?'*

That is the last we hear of Caratacus. Was he a British hero, or something less? He did well to survive, farce or no farce. Tacitus's narrative now returns to events in Britain.

Caratacus was certainly not being missed by the Silures, or anyone else in that area. In fact, things were not looking at all good in the province, from the Roman point of view.

> *But now his* [Ostorius's] *success, hitherto unblemished, began to waver. Possibly the elimination of Caratacus had caused a slackening of energy, in the belief that the war was over. Or perhaps the enemy's sympathy with their great king had whetted their appetite for revenge. In Silurian country, Roman troops left to build forts under a divisional chief of staff were surrounded, and only saved from annihilation because neighbouring fortresses learnt of their siege and speedily sent help. As it was, casualties included the chief of staff, eight company-commanders, and the pick of the men. Shortly afterwards a Roman foraging party was put to flight. So were cavalry troops sent to its rescue. Ostorius threw in his light auxiliary battalions, but even so did not check the rout until the regular brigades*

joined in. Their strength made the struggle equal and eventually gave us the advantage. However, night was coming on, so the enemy escaped almost undamaged.

This also sounds as though it might have come from an unknown soldier's memoirs.

It is interesting that Ostorius was having a fort built not very far away from existing ones. Presumably he is trying to contain the Silures by making a close-knit chain of them. That is all very well, but each fort must be provisioned and manned with enough troops to keep it secure and deal with raiding parties, which of course cuts down the strength of the mobile supporting fighting force, and that mobile supporting force was being kept busy apparently.

Battle followed battle. They were mostly guerrilla fights, in woods and bogs. Some were accidental – the results of chance encounters. Others were planned with calculated bravery. The motives were hatred or plunder. Sometimes these engagements were ordered by the generals; sometimes they knew nothing of them.

The Silures were exceptionally stubborn. They were enraged by a much-repeated saying of the Roman commander that they must be utterly exterminated, just as the Sugambri had once been annihilated or transplanted to the Gallic provinces.

Two auxiliary battalions, which their greedy commanders had taken plundering with insufficient precautions, fell into a trap laid by the Silures.

Then they began, by gifts of spoils and prisoners, to tempt other tribes to join their rebellion.

Things were clearly getting out of hand, and it was all too much for poor Ostorius.

At this point, exhausted by his anxious responsibilities, Ostorius died. The enemy exulted that so considerable a general, if not defeated in battle, had at least been eliminated by warfare.

On hearing of the governor's death the emperor, not wanting to leave the province masterless, appointed Aulus Didius Gallus to take over. Didius made for Britain rapidly. But he found a further deterioration. For in the interval a Roman brigade commanded by Mantius Valens had suffered a reverse. Reports were magnified – the enemy magnified them, to frighten the new general; and the general magnified them to increase his glory if he won, and improve his excuse if resistance proved unbreakable. Again the damage was due to the Silures; until deterred by Didius' arrival, they plundered far and wide.

Didius was obviously another who was ready to play the spin doctoring propaganda game. They all seem to have been at it. The chains of Roman forts were not doing much good either, from the sounds of it. Perhaps the XXth legion had had too many green recruits in its ranks, or the years of garrison duty in Camulodunum had drained their aggressive fighting spirit, or possibly the Silures had too much of what they lacked.

Tacitus now has an interesting story to tell us about the Brigantes. It comes, surprisingly enough, from his other great work – the *Histories*. It should not have been there since that book was supposed to cover the years from AD68, but since this passage repeats some of the things Tacitus has already told us, he obviously got it out of its correct chronological sequence and thence into the wrong book.

> . . . *and the spate of rumours about civil war emboldened the Britons to pluck up their courage and follow a man called Venutius, who, quite apart from a violent character and a hatred of all things Roman, was goaded to fury by a personal feud with Queen Cartimandua. She had been for some time ruler of the Brigantes, and was a princess of high birth and hence influence. This she had increased thanks to her treacherous capture of King Caratacus, an action by which she was generally thought to have set the seal upon Claudius' triumph. Hence came wealth and the self-indulgence of prosperity. She tired of Venutius, who was her consort, and gave her hand and kingdom to his armour bearer, one Vellocatus. This scandal immediately shook the royal house to its foundations. The discarded husband could rely on the support of the Brigantian people, the lover upon the infatuation of the queen and her ruthless cruelty. So Venutius summoned help from outside, and a simultaneous revolt on the part of the Brigantes themselves reduced Cartimandua to a position of acute danger, in which she appealed for Roman assistance. In the event, our cohorts and cavalry regiments did succeed, at the cost of desperate fighting, in rescuing the queen from a tight corner. Venutius inherited the throne, and we the fighting.*

Real soap opera stuff, isn't it? But who really won? If the Roman troops merely rescued Cartimandua from a tight corner, leaving Venutius to inherit the throne, it rather looks as though Venutius did.

Tacitus now tells most of that story again, in the *Annals*:

> *However, since Caratacus' capture the best strategist was Venutius, who as I mentioned earlier, was a Brigantian. While married to the tribal queen, Cartimandua, he had remained loyal and under Roman protection. But divorce had immediately been followed by hostilities against her and then against us. At first, the Brigantes had merely fought among themselves. Cartimandua had astutely trapped Venutius' brother and other relatives. But her enemies, infuriated and goaded by fears of humiliating feminine rule,*

invaded her kingdom with a powerful force of picked warrors. We had foreseen this, and sent auxiliary battalions to support her. The engagement that followed had no positive results at first but ended more favourably. A battle fought by a regular brigade under Caesius Nasica likewise had a satisfactory ending. Didius, of impressive seniority and incapacitated by age, was content to act through subordinates and on the defensive.

(These campaigns were conducted by two imperial governors over a period of years. But I have described them in one place since piecemeal description would cast a strain on the memory. Now I return to the chronological succession of events.)

Tacitus acknowledges here the difficulty of dealing with widespread matters chronologically. His solution of describing them 'all in one place' may well occur in a different context later on.

Maps generally place the Brigantes tribe on, and to both sides of the Pennines, which is surprising, because in later history the Pennines were a divider of communities, not a link between them. Where Cartimandua's palace actually was is not known for certain, but it was possibly east of the Pennines, near York, which was where Peddars Way headed, having passed just north of Lincoln, but there might of course have been another palace on the western side, near Manchester. Tacitus goes on, in his *Agricola* this time:

Didius Gallus . . . kept a firm hold on what his predecessors had won, and even pushed some few forts into outlying districts, so that he could say that he had extended his sphere of duty.

Veranius succeeded Didius, only to die within the year. After him, Suetonius Paulinus enjoyed two years of success, conquering tribes and establishing strong forts.

Tacitus also covers the same period in the *Annals*:

The imperial governor Aulus Didius Gallus had, as I have said, merely held his own. His successor Quintus Veranius had only conducted minor raids against the Silures when death terminated his operations. His life had been famous for its austerity. But his testamentary last words were glaringly self-seeking, for they grossly flattered Nero and added that Veranius, if he had lived two years longer, would have presented him with the whole province

Tacitus states that forts were still being built to contain the frontier tribes.

An examination of the map showing the sites of the known 'Claudio-Neronian' forts ought to indicate where rebel activity had been most strong. It is surprising then to note that, in spite of all the recorded Silurian incidents, there are few forts actually in Wales.

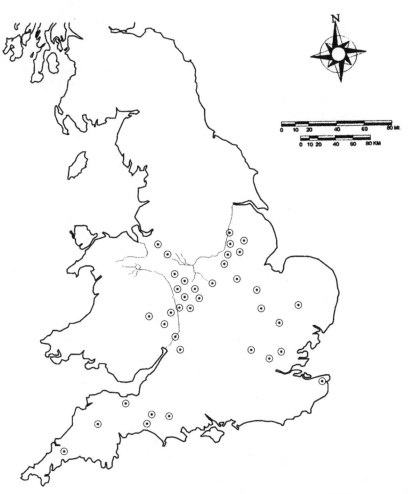

PROBABLE SITES OF CLAUDIO-NERONIAN FORTS
AD 43 TO AD 60

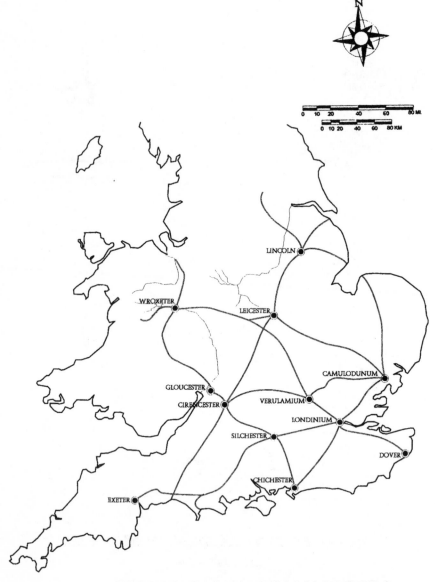

PROBABLE MAIN ROMAN ROADS
CIRCA AD 60

On the line of the Severn and thence on towards the Mersey, there are thirteen forts, excluding the legionary headquarters. Only five of these confront Silurian territory, and four seem more concerned with the Midlands than Wales and may therefore be earlier rather than later in date, or just store houses and granaries. In Devon and Cornwall there are five forts, while along the Trent there are seven.

It would seem then that circa AD60, each legion, in addition to its headquarters or base camp, was manning an average of six forts, which were strung out in a very erratic line some miles to the north-west of the Fosse Way. Ignoring auxiliaries, if half of a legion's infantry, say 3,000, remained in reserve at its base camp, then each fort may have been manned by as many as 500 troops. Some forts would be bigger than others of course, but that does seem rather a large average garrison size. A lower figure might have been expected – two or three hundred at the most, but perhaps there are sites yet to be discovered.

We had worked out earlier which main roads may have been built during the first four years of the Roman occupation. During the next thirteen years more would obviously have been constructed. Many of the later forts built to contain the Welsh were probably sited much nearer to Wales itself, and thus too far from the Fosse Way for that still to have been a fully effective communicating link. So a new road was probably built, passing much closer to all those front line forts, linking Gloucester in the south directly with Wroxeter, then going on to service a few forts on the way towards the Mersey.

With the IInd legion having been transferred to the west country the road from Camulodunum to Londinium was probably extended west to Silchester, then via Old Sarum, to Dorchester, and linked through Axminster with Exeter. A road may also have been built from Londinium to Chichester, and Chichester itself linked via Silchester with Cirencester.

There may, of course, have been many other roads built for domestic convenience, but those thirteen years had seen a lot of rebel activity, and the war-like tribes on the frontiers had still not been subdued, so it is very possible that the legions restricted the building of additional communication links to those that were military necessities.

The Romans had then been in southern Britain nearly seventeen years. There may have been trouble occasionally on its borders, but in the settled areas the British may have seemed to the Roman authorities suitably cowed, and unlikely to cause any serious problems, however they were treated. If that was their opinion, they were seriously mistaken. The Boudicca rebellion was about to break, and set most of the province into turmoil.

CHAPTER VII

The Roman Attack on Anglesey

AD60 – the year of Queen Boudicca's rebellion. Dio breaks off from relating a rather silly story about Nero's prize-wining lyre playing, and writes:

> *While this sort of child's play was going on at Rome, a terrible disaster occurred in Britain. Two cities were sacked, eighty thousand of the Romans and of their allies perished, and the island was lost to Rome.*

The latter claim is obviously somewhat exaggerated, but it is certainly a more dramatic opening to the saga of Boudicca's rebellion than Tacitus reports. He starts his account in the *Annals* with:

> *The following year, when the consuls were Lucius Caesennius Paetus and Publius Petronius Turpilianus, witnessed a serious disaster in Britain.*

He then goes on to outline the background to the event by having a few digs at those who were governors before Suetonius Paulinus, which we read in the previous chapter, but he then continues:

> *The new imperial governor was Gaius Suetonius Paulinus. Corbulo's rival in military science, as in popular talk – which makes everybody complete – he was ambitious to achieve victories as glorious as the reconquest of Armenia. So Suetonius planned to attack the island of Mona [Anglesey], which although thickly populated had also given sanctuary to many refugees.*

Corbulo was a man of high military repute in Rome, so Suetonius had obviously already made himself a reputation with his exploits in Armenia. Tacitus rather gives the impression here that Suetonius had only just taken over the province, and that the attack on Anglesey was his first notable achievement, but he has already told us that Suetonius had had two years of success in Britain, building forts and conquering tribes. Those two years would have given him plenty of time to plant his feet firmly under the table, and to have met, and presumably got to know, all the important people in the province, including the client kings and other tribal chieftains.

The island of Mona is assumed to be Anglesey, even though it is evident that both Caesar and Dio Cassius believed Mona to be the Isle of Man. However, when we come to read Tacitus's account, it is quite clear that he was referring to an island near enough to the mainland for the channel between to be forded. The Isle of Man is much too far away for that to be possible, so there appears to be no other sensible alternative. Anglesey it must have been. Tacitus, from the *Agricola* this time:

> . . . *Suetonius Paulinus enjoyed two years of success, conquering tribes and establishing strong forts. Emboldened thereby to attack the island of Anglesey, which was feeding the native resistance, he exposed himself to a stab in the back.*

Suetonius stands high in Tacitus's esteem, perhaps because he was an early patron of his father in-law, as is acknowledged. The *Agricola* again:

> *He* [Agricola] *served his apprenticeship in the army to the satisfaction of Suetonius Paulinus, that sound and thorough general, and was picked by him to be tried out on his staff. Neither before nor since has Britain ever been in a more uneasy or dangerous state. Veterans were butchered, colonies burned to the ground, armies isolated. We had to fight for life before we could think of victory.*

And just in case we had formed the opinion that it might really have been Agricola who won this war, Tacitus puts us right.

> *The campaign, of course, was conducted under the strategy and leadership of another, and the decisive success and the credit for recovering Britain fell to the General.*

We are told that Anglesey was attacked because it had '. . . given sanctuary to many refugees', and because it was '. . . feeding the native resistance'. The first possibility was considered when discussing Caratacus's activities. The second reason has often been taken literally, as meaning that Anglesey was supplying food to dissidents on the mainland. That may well have been true, but those words can also be interpreted as meaning that it was a place where groups of rebels were instructed and trained in the arts of hit and run warfare, and then were fed back into Wales to renew the resistance movement. Which is perhaps why, after so many campaigns *conquering tribes*, the Romans had still not quelled the opposition.

Some authorities claim that the Druids were the implacable enemies of Rome, and organised all the rebellions and resistance movements from Anglesey, which was supposedly their headquarters. They maintain that Suetonius needed to destroy the Druids' influence there before peace could reign in the province, and they also suggest that the Boudicca rebellion may have occurred for no other reason than to distract Suetonius and his army from that purpose.

There is no evidence in our sources to support such propositions, but the concept has become a popular theory, and we therefore ought to devote a little time to discussing it in more detail.

Suetonius would probably have made his plans for this offensive against Anglesey during the previous winter. No one outside his top war committee, if he had one, should have had the slightest idea where Suetonius's main aggressive activity would fall during AD60.

However, we can probably be certain that at the start of each campaigning season there would have been plenty of sharp-eyed British watchers, observing the movements of the Roman troops from a safe distance – because for nigh on sixteen years, at that time of the year a Roman army had set off to pillage, plunder or lay to waste the territories of the Dumnonii, the Silures, the Cornovii or Ordovices, or even the half-friendly Brigantes. All those tribes must have been wondering where the blow would fall that year. Unfortunately for them the Romans would have known that they were being watched, and because there was small profit in going straight to those areas where the population and the booty had already been evacuated, their routes would have been deliberately circuitous. So the British watchers would only have known for certain what was in the wind when those troops actually turned up at the Menai Straits.

Would there have been time for a messenger to get from Anglesey to the east of England, as those who support the Druid conspiracy theory suggest, with the exhortation: 'For heaven's sake stir up some trouble to draw this lot away, or else we Druids are lost'? And if such a message had been sent, would there have been time for the east of England to have organised an adequate diversion? Probably not. Anyway, why would that message have been sent to the far away east of England, when the Silures or Brigantes were much nearer to Anglesey, and could thus have responded sooner and more effectively?

The theory of a Druid master plan is highly speculative. If the Druids were such a major thorn in the side of the Romans, then surely previous governors would have done something about them long before. In Tacitus's account of the battle of Mona, which comes next, the Druids are mentioned just once, and it is the only reference he ever makes to them, and Dio ignores them completely.

There are other reasons for the rebellion that are far more substantial than the Druid proposition, so let us get back to the main story, which at the moment is the attack on Anglesey. Tacitus, in the *Annals*:

> *Flat-bottomed boats were built to contend with the shifting shallows, and these took the infantry across. Then came the cavalry; some utilised fords, but in deeper water the men swam beside their horses. The enemy lined the shore in a dense armed mass. Among them were black-robed women with dishevelled hair like Furies, brandishing torches. Close by stood Druids, raising their hands to heaven and screaming dreadful curses.*
>
> *This weird spectacle awed the Roman soldiers into a sort of paralysis. They stood still – and presented themselves as a target. But then they urged each other (and were urged by the general) not to fear a horde of fanatical women. Onward pressed their standards and they bore down their opponents, enveloping them in the flames of their own torches.*

The crossing was presumably made near to the Menai Straits. With sea levels supposedly lower then, one might have thought that it was possible to cross at low tide without the need for boats and swimming. As a military manoeuvre, the attack, as it is described, seems rather crude. To cross where a defensive force is ready and alert, would be to risk heavy casualties. Perhaps many of those boats and swimming horses were used by troops crossing somewhere out of sight of the gesticulating Britons. Then that business about the Roman soldiers 'presenting themselves as targets', makes more sense – if they were really drawing the attention of the defending British to themselves, while other troops crossed unopposed elsewhere with the intention of surprising the Britons with attacks on their flanks and rear. The Roman navy almost certainly had a part to play, but we are not told what it was – diversionary landings on other parts of the island perhaps.

The numbers of Roman troops involved are not mentioned either. We can only guess at this point that Suetonius's field army was probably made up of large detachments from the two legions confronting, and nearest, to that area of Wales, namely the XIVth legion, and the XXth. An effective fighting force, one would suppose, would at least be legion-sized – say 5,000 or 6,000 first line infantry legionaries, plus, of course, those very flexible and reliable auxiliaries and cavalry, who are rarely named or numbered.

It would appear then, that the Romans had convincingly defeated the Britons at the battle of Anglesey. What happened next?

Tacitus states in the *Annals*:

> *Suetonius garrisoned the conquered island. The groves devoted to Mona's barbarous superstitions he demolished. For it was their religion to drench their altars in the blood of prisoners and consult their gods by means of human entrails.*

Nasty, but then the Romans were hardly more civilised when it came to savage cruelty. At least the British do not seem to have practised it merely for public entertainment.

Dio says much the same as Tacitus, without the entrails:

> *Now it chanced that Paulinus had already brought Mona to terms . . .*

But had he? Having told us in the *Annals* that 'Suetonius garrisoned the conquered island', Tacitus blatantly contradicts himself in a story which he tells much later, in his *Agricola*, when his father-in-law had become governor of Britain:

> He [Agricola] *decided, therefore, to reduce the island of Anglesey, from the occupation of which Paulinus had been recalled by the revolt of all Britain.*

So, if Suetonius did put a garrison into Anglesey, then he must soon have withdrawn it. Tacitus tells us why in the *Annals*:

> *While Suetonius was thus occupied, he learnt of a sudden rebellion in the province.*

Dio:

> *. . . and so on learning of the disaster in Britain he at once set sail thither from Mona.*

Tacitus, in the *Agricola*:

> *In fact, had not Paulinus, on hearing of the revolt, made speed to help, Britain would have been lost.*

Some messenger, or even possibly messengers, had come hot foot to Suetonius with a tale of woe. We do not know what those messages actually said, or who they came from, but the news must have been pretty bad to get such an immediate reaction. Dio says Suetonius acted 'at once', and Tacitus says he 'made speed'.

So far, so good. Our interest has been aroused and the tension heightened, but unfortunately both Dio and Tacitus now switch their narratives to the east of England, to explain how the rebellion started, leaving us still wondering what Suetonius was going to do next.

It is their story, and this is the way they want to tell it, so, to prevent confusion we will have to come back to Suetonius later, when we have learned just what had been going on elsewhere.

CHAPTER VIII

The Iceni Uprising

Dio and Tacitus now enter into lengthy explanations of what, in their individual opinions, were the causes of the revolt. This is Tacitus's account in the *Annals*:

> *Prasutagus, king of the Iceni, after a life of long and renowned prosperity, had made the emperor co-heir with his own two daughters. Prasutagus hoped by this submissiveness to preserve his Kingdom and household from attack. But it turned out otherwise. Kingdom and household alike were plundered like prizes of war, the one by Roman officers, the other by Roman slaves. As a beginning, his widow Boudicca was flogged and their daughters raped. The Icenian chiefs were deprived of their hereditary estates as if the Romans had been given the whole country. The king's own relatives were treated like slaves.*
>
> *And the humiliated Iceni feared still worse, now that they had been reduced to provincial status. So they rebelled.*

We are told that Prasutagus was wealthy and prosperous, so it is understandable that his estate might have attracted the attention of the Roman tax men when he died, but why, after seventeen years of co-operation with the Romans, were the Iceni being reduced to the status of a conquered people? And why all the rough stuff? If Prasutagus tried to preserve his kingdom by drafting his will in that particular fashion, then he may have been forewarned that there might be trouble when he died. Perhaps Prasutagus had become inefficient or unco-operative to such an extent that the Roman authorities had already decided that the Iceni's client king status would not be allowed to continue. Perhaps it was simply because Prasutagus had no apparent direct male heir to become a safe pro-Roman administrator. Even so, it seems strange that the whole tribal administrative structure was being torn apart, with chiefs losing their hereditary estates and royal relatives being treated as slaves.

Perhaps the Romans had decided to set up a *colonia* on Iceni lands, similar to the one at Camulodunum. There are field systems on the north Norfolk coast near Thornham which match well with the standard size of land grant given to veteran legionaries, and so a colony may indeed have been created in that area at some time. That might explain the large-scale sequestration of Iceni land, but there is nothing in our sources to support the idea, and anyway, it is difficult to believe that the Romans could have expected to achieve that without trouble. When the colony at Camulodunum was set up, the Romans had practically the whole of the XXth legion on hand to keep the already weakened Trinovantes in check. One would have thought that at the least a similar number of troops would have been necessary to keep the still largely independent Iceni in order.

The Roman officials sent to the Iceni capital would not have been responsible to Suetonius the governor, but to Catus Decianus, who was the province's Rome-appointed procurator. He was a top civil servant, whose administrative responsibilities were probably similar to those of our tax-gathering Chancellor of the Exchequer. He would probably never have had direct control over any of the regular legions.

However, before we deliberate further on the actions of Decianus and his officials, there are significant factors yet to be revealed in Dio's account.

Dio comes up with some explanations that Tacitus presumably did not even know about, for if he had, he would surely have used them. It also shows that Dio did not simply copy or slavishly follow Tacitus's works. He obviously did some research of his own, and he may have found, in Rome's archives, Decianus's actual report to Nero justifying his actions 'Decianus . . . maintained', Dio says in this next passage.

> An excuse for the war was found in the confiscation of the sums of money that Claudius had given to the foremost Britons; for these sums, as Decianus Catus, the procurator of the island, maintained, were to be paid back. This was one reason for the uprising; another was found in the fact that Seneca (a multi-millionaire, Nero's one-time tutor and a member of Rome's high society), in the hope of receiving a good rate of interest, had lent to the islanders 40,000,000 sesterces that they did not want, and had afterwards called in this loan all at once and had resorted to severe measures in exacting it.

So it would appear that Claudius, back in AD43, had originally bribed the foremost British kings and chieftains into their farcical submissions with gifts of money, that Decianus understood, or had been instructed by Nero to claim, were not really gifts at all, but loans which were repayable on demand. Presumably then it was not just Prasutagus and the Iceni who were affected, since Dio says 'sums . . . given to the foremost Britons' and similarly that Seneca's loans were made to the 'islanders', although how Seneca could lend money to people who did not want to borrow is difficult to comprehend.

Presumably Decianus was acting as Seneca's agent as well as in his official capacity, and if his collectors had been roaming throughout the settled areas of the province, gathering in with heavy official hands disputable debts that were anyway so old they'd been forgotten about, and, no doubt, adding on heavy cumulative interest charges, then it would hardly be surprising if there was discontent among the Britons throughout the whole province. We are not talking about only the tribal chieftains being put under financial pressure. If those chiefs needed to get their hands on large sums of cash quickly, then much of it would almost certainly have been extracted from their own subjects in some way. Nothing hurts more, even in this day and age, than being hit in the pocket by a ruthless officialdom that has all the weight of law enforcers standing by with truncheons drawn. The blood boils rebelliously just at the thought of it. Maybe it did so back in AD60.

All this would have hit the Iceni particularly badly. Not only would Decianus's men have been clawing back Claudius's gift and Seneca's loan, but at the same time, because of Prasutagus's untimely death, if what Tacitus says is also true, they would have been after at least half of that dead king's estate as well. Would there have been any of Prasutagus's wealth left after all that had been extracted?

Dio's words, 'had resorted to severe measures in exacting it', must surely mean that the bailiffs were going in to seize goods to the value of the debts, and probably using force and violence as well. In which case one can understand Iceni tempers, and the tempers of others in the province flaring up too.

It is possible that Prasutagus was still alive when Decianus's officials turned up demanding the immediate repayment of Claudius's and Seneca's loans. Faced with financial ruin, the strain may have brought on a heart attack. That might account for the Romans not having an armed escort adequate for the task they appear to have set themselves.

Decianus's staff would probably have been recruited from retired regular officers, and if they were from the XXth legion, one can understand the ready use of the heavy hand. The 'Roman slaves' would have been the educated clerks, who no doubt did all the real accounting work.

Nero was always short of money, and Britain may not have been turning out to be such a ready source of funds as Rome had originally hoped. Of one thing we can be reasonably sure – Decianus would have been under constant imperial pressure to improve his cash flow. When the riches of the wealthy King Prasutagus thus came suddenly into the orbit of death duties and inheritance taxes, regardless of other considerations, Decianus must have been over the moon. It would have seemed a god-given opportunity to get his hands on some really substantial funds, and get central office off his back for a while. Possibly as soon as he heard of

Prasutagus's regrettable demise, he ordered his tax collectors to get their hands on anything of realisable value that could even remotely be assumed part of the dead man's wealth, on the basis of grab now, and if necessary, argue later. Other than land and livestock, the tangible wealth of those days was not verifiable share certificates and black figures on bank statements, but coinage, jewellery and other valuable bits and pieces, all of which are easily hidden.

More gold torcs and similar artefacts have been found in Norfolk than probably anywhere else in Britain. Many of those items were apparently made well before AD60, so they could have been part of the contents of Prasutagus's treasure chests, which may have been buried secretly by his immediate household, under a floor in a royal residence perhaps, as part of a concerted, and possibly successful attempt to ensure that as little of it as possible actually found its way into Roman imperial hands. It may be that when Decianus's men searched through Prasutagus's palace there was little of value left to loot and plunder.

That would have put them seriously on the spot. Living as Decianus did, under the pressures of a tyrant like Nero, he would need to be a tyrant himself to his underlings, and they would need to be tyrannical too, in the carrying out of their duties. So, in the process of trying to find out where all Prasutagus's treasure had gone, Decianus's collectors may have gone over the top with the bully boy tactics on Prasutagus's family, friends and palace staff; particularly the female members. That might explain the use of the words 'flogging' and 'rape'.

However, the Iceni palace routines would probably not have disintegrated or fragmented just because the King had died. There would still have been guards and other officials about, even a chief of police, if there was one. It is difficult to imagine that those people would not have reacted aggressively if the royal family and the palace womenfolk, whom they were there to protect, were molested by strangers, and started screaming for help.

A quick punch-up – the flash of a knife or a sword, and what began as an 'incident', would suddenly be an 'affray'. Add a few badly injured Romans, and the 'affray' would have developed into 'armed resistance'. Then, if a few of the Iceni chiefs and their followers, whose hereditary estates were also being confiscated, rode in from out of town, all wild and angry and shouting, 'They'll get my lands over my dead body!', and one of the tax-gatherers' Roman escorts had duly obliged, then the 'armed resistance' would have progressed into a 'revolt' and then, because they'd already gone too far to step back, into a full scale 'rebellion'.

That may be a fair thumb-nail sketch of how the Iceni rebellion started, or it may not, but the real cause must surely have been the severe measures adopted by Decianus's officials.

Of course, if Decianus was merely carring out orders given to him by

Nero in Rome, then it is not surprising that both he and Suetonius seem to have got away with what can only be described as a sloppy bit of maladministration. But government offices, whether in Westminster or ancient Rome, never make mistakes or take the blame. They apply the thirty-year secrecy rule on all the documents in their archives, and push such things under the carpet so that nothing becomes public knowledge while the government ministers are still alive. That might be the reason why Tacitus does not appear to have seen source material which a hundred odd years later might have been readily available to Dio. Anyway, the fact was that Decianus had stirred up a hornets' nest in the Iceni lands, and discontent was probably also rife elsewhere in the province.

We may reasonably suppose that, under normal circumstances, if either of the client kings, or any other of the important tribal chieftains, were faced with a situation they considered unfair or unreasonable, they would have been able to make representations and protestations on the matter directly to the highest authority in Britain, namely Nero's representative – the governor Suetonius. However, Suetonius would not have been available to receive any such protests. 'He is unfortunately away at the moment, and we don't know when he will be back,' the *aides-de-camp* in his office might have explained, before they went on to say that the governor would undoubtedly have sympathised and understood their problems, but that nothing could be done in his absence.

Now here is an interesting proposition. Suetonius must have known that Decianus was going to be clawing back those Claudian gifts and Seneca loans that spring or early summer, and that it would almost certainly result in high-level protests from the British chiefs. Could that be the real reason why Suetonius took himself off to remote Anglesey – a place no other governor had been particularly bothered about during the past seventeen years – just to get himself well out of the way of an irritating and embarrassing situation? Even today the accountant's debt collection and cash flow problems are anathema to those who specialise in sales, production or any other more material discipline. Possibly Suetonius's practical military mind felt the same way about Decianus's financial problems. It may be a simplistic proposition, but it nevertheless reflects human nature. If Suetonius went to Anglesey for that reason, then he was guilty of a grievous misjudgement. Had he been in his province, where he probably should have been, he might have been able to deal better with the events that followed Prasutagus's unexpected death, and matters might not have got out of hand. But he wasn't, and he didn't, and matters did get out of hand, because the Iceni found themselves cornered, with their backs to the wall and nowhere to go, so they rebelled.

Dio has this to say about the leader of the rebellion:

Moreover, all this ruin was brought upon the Romans by a woman, a fact which itself caused them the greatest shame . . . But the person who was chiefly instrumental in rousing the natives and persuading them to fight the Romans, the person who was thought worthy to be their leader and who directed the conduct of the entire war, was Boudicca, a Briton woman of the royal family and possessed of greater intelligence than often belongs to women.

The dominant male attitude of the Romans, and the Greeks, does rather tend to support the theory that Prasutagus's failure to have a direct male heir might have doomed the Icenis' special relationship with the Roman administration. Dio continues:

This woman assembled her army, to the number of some 120,000, and then ascended a tribunal which had been constructed of earth in the Roman fashion. In stature she was very tall, in appearance most terrifying, in the glance of her eye most fierce, and her voice was harsh; a great mass of the tawniest hair fell to her hips; around her neck was a large golden necklace; and she wore a tunic of divers colours over which a thick mantle was fastened with a brooch. This was her invariable attire. She now grasped a spear to aid her in terrifying all beholders and spoke as follows . . .

This is a description with enough detail in it to suggest that it might well be accurately sourced, but the speech which follows indubitably comes from the mind of Dio Cassius. It tells us nothing about the way the rebellion developed, so it can be read in full in the Appendix.

Tacitus now takes the story off at a tangent yet again. He has already moved us from Anglesey to Norfolk, now it seems we must move again, to Essex this time.

CHAPTER IX

The Attack on Colchester

Instead of expounding on what the Iceni did to develop their revolt into a general uprising, Tacitus takes us seventy or eighty miles farther south, to Camulodunum. In the *Annals* he says:

> With them [the Iceni] *rose the Trinovantes and others. Servitude had not broken them, and they had secretly plotted together to become free again.*

In his account of the reasons for the Iceni revolt Tacitus had certainly led us to believe that the rebellion was a spontaneous reaction to unexpected events. He told us that '. . . the humiliated Iceni feared still worse, now that they had been reduced to provincial status. So they rebelled.' Now he is saying that it had all been secretly planned beforehand. Both statements cannot be right. One would have thought that any plots involving Prasutagus would have come to a sudden end, or been seriously delayed or disrupted when he died – unless it was Boudicca who had been doing the intriguing. Anyway, if the plotting was secret, how could Tacitus or the Romans have ever learned of it? His 'secretly plotted' might simply be an example of misreporting, if several tribal leaders had tried to make a joint protest to Suetonius about Decianus's activities, which is only what one would have expected them to do under the circumstances. Tacitus again, in the *Annals*:

> They particularly hated the Roman ex-soldiers who had recently established a settlement at Camulodunum. The settlers drove the Trinovantes from their homes and land, and called them prisoners and slaves. The troops encouraged the settlers' outrages, since their own way of behaving was the same – and they looked forward to similar licence for themselves. Moreover, the temple erected to the divine Claudius was a blatant stronghold of alien rule, and its observances were a pretext to make the natives appointed as its priests drain the whole country dry.

Tacitus uses the phrase 'They particularly hated'. Those words seem to imply that the Iceni hated the Roman colonists in Camulodunum as fervently as did the Trinovantes, but is that really likely – or indeed what Tacitus actually meant?

Having voluntarily accepted Roman rule, the Iceni had presumably been living reasonably contentedly for the past seventeen years under their king, Prasutagus. His client king status must have meant that any Roman presence in their tribal lands was relatively low-key and benign. So why should the Iceni have particularly hated the faraway Roman colonists in Camulodunum, who had done their tribe no harm and with whom they probably had never had contact?

In this passage Tacitus is probably relating only the viewpoint of those Trinovantes living in the Camulodunum area. His words can be read that way if you want them to, and it probably makes more sense to do so. Frankly, he sounds somewhat confused at this point in his story. His comment about natives being appointed priests of a Roman temple is probably extremely unlikely, but that the burden of provisioning or stocking up the cellars should somehow fall on the Trinovantes, probably isn't – if that is what he means by draining 'the whole country dry'.

The fate of Camulodunum forms a significant part of Tacitus's story now, and so perhaps we should try to work out what had been going on in that *colonia* since it had been set up twelve years earlier. Tacitus makes it pretty clear that the settlers and local troops were abusing their powers, and he hints that it should not have been like that. So, did the local Roman troops and the XXth legion veterans do much as they liked in Camulodunum, while their officers and the authorities turned a blind eye?

This is what Tacitus wrote about the XXth legion in his *Agricola* when, some years later, his father-in-law was its commander:

> As a matter of fact, the legion was a problem and a menace even to consular legates, so naturally its legate, being merely of praetorian rank, was impotent to control it; perhaps he was to blame, perhaps his troops were. Agricola was thus chosen, not merely to succeed, but to punish. But he showed a rare self-denial; he let it appear that he had found in his legion the loyalty he created.

A problem and a menace were they? Their commanders were impotent to control them?

Well, with several thousand of those sorts of characters roaming about, Camulodunum, even if it did have some sort of fancy senate house, bath house, forum, theatre and temple, would not have been a place where a self-respecting Trinovante, or anyone else for that matter, would have wanted to wander far abroad after dark. At the risk of labouring the point, there are still further implications to be drawn from the XXth's unruly behaviour

It is not unreasonable to suppose that the toga-clad Tacitus type of Roman citizen, who lived in the capital, would have preferred to spend his days in the company of like-minded, educated people, indulging in polite conversation while they lounged in the hot room of the bath house, discussing current affairs or interesting theoretical propositions. Such people would not have mixed well with the tough, ill-disciplined ex-troopers, either socially, or in the council chamber. Yet as *bone fide* Roman citizens and payers of community taxes, the ex-soldiers would surely have had just as much right to be heard in the forum as anyone else, unless – because their farms were outside the city boundaries – they were not entitled to such privileges, and thus had no say in the running of its affairs. If that were the case then those veterans, who had been settled there specifically to help defend the city, would have had a far more justifiable excuse to be discontented and unruly. Different outlooks on life would have meant different priorities in any proposals for developing the city. If money was being spent on fancy amenities rather than on urgently needed defensive measures, some of those ex-soldiers might well have said, in Latin of course, 'When it all goes wrong I'm not going to risk my neck fighting for those stupid fools', or words to that effect.

This is not just pure speculation. What Tacitus says next does illustrate confusion in Camulodunum's civic development. The *Annals*:

> *It seemed easy to destroy the settlement; for it had no walls. That was a matter which Roman commanders, thinking of amenities rather than needs, had neglected.*

No walls after seventeen years? That is dreadful. Of course there would obviously have been a properly walled wooden fort there originally, but perhaps its defences had been dismantled to make room for those amenities, and nothing had been put in their place. Presumably Suetonius and Decianus must bear some responsibility for what was going on in their capital city, but most likely the local commander was one of those politically appointed tribunes or legates with little or no practical military experience, but lots of old school or family clout. Whoever he was, he did not even react sensibly when it became clear that trouble was brewing, but maybe if you weren't into tarot cards, weegee boards or reading entrails, it wasn't all that clear that danger did loom. In the *Annals* Tacitus says:

> *At this juncture, for no visible reason, the statue of Victory at Camulodunum fell down – with its back turned as though it was fleeing the enemy. Delirious women chanted of destruction at hand. They cried that in the local senate-house outlandish yells had been heard; the theatre had echoed with shrieks; at the mouth of the Thames a phantom settlement had been seen in ruins. A blood-red colour in the sea, too, and shapes like human corpses*

left by the ebb tide, were interpreted hopefully by the Britons – and with
terror by the settlers.

Dio says much the same:

Indeed, Heaven gave them indications of the catastrophe beforehand. For at
night there was heard to issue from the senate-house foreign jargon mingled
with laughter, and from the theatre outcries and lamentations, though no
mortal man had uttered the words or the groans; houses were seen under the
water in the river Thames, and the ocean between the island and Gaul once
grew blood-red at flood tide.

There is nothing that Dio or Tacitus have yet said to suggest that anyone
in Camulodunum knew about the rebellion of the Iceni, or that the
Trinovantes were also in revolt, both of which would have been more
tangible reasons for creating terror among the inhabitants than the
accounts just quoted. Perhaps their dread was then just a widespread
apprehension and nervous tension caused by Decianus's debt collecting
activities.

However, the city authorities did do something more practical than
merely quake with fear over strange omens. They tried to pass the buck,
and some of the responsibility for the defence of their city, to someone
else. Tacitus, in the *Annals*:

Suetonius, however, was far away. So they appealed for help to the imperial
agent Catus Decianus. He sent them barely two hundred men, incompletely
armed. There was also a small garrison on the spot. Reliance was placed on
the temple's protection. Misled by secret pro-rebels, who hampered their
plans, they dispensed with rampart or trench. They omitted also to evacuate
old people and women and thus leave only fighting men behind. Their
precautions were appropriate to a time of unbroken peace.

Presumably Catus Decianus was not in Camulodunum at that time. If he
was in Londinium or Verulamium then it would have taken several days
for his two hundred men to march to the capital, but the big question
surely must be, why, with three thousand or so veteran troops on hand to
defend the city, did they need to ask for anyone's help?

What comes over reasonably clearly is that there seems to have been
ample time to prepare the city better for a siege and also to vastly
improve its defences. The veterans had been used to building forts, and
throwing up adequate walls and ramparts whenever they made camp for
the night, and one would have thought they could have created
something similar, or even better, for the city, if they had been given the
chance. But presumably they were not, since rampart and trench were

dispensed with. Perhaps creating better defences might have damaged those precious amenities in some way, and was thus forbidden. Or was it that the veteran settlers had already refused to co-operate with plans for the defence of the city that seemed to their experienced and war-trained minds a complete waste of time? With their reputation the XXth veterans would certainly not have suffered fools gladly, whoever they were, and the reliance on the temple's protection, if that meant having faith in their gods rather than in the unlikely possibility that it was a defensible fortress-like structure, does sound a bit pathetic. So, had those veterans already decided that the city could not be defended, and were going to march away and abandon it? Was that why Decianus's help was being sought?

The Roman commander in charge of the defence of Camulodunum certainly seems to have had his head well and truly in the clouds. His military incompetence seems hardly believable, but not so many years ago a high ranking general refused to allow trenches to be dug to defend the island of Singapore, reputedly because it would have been bad for morale. That was, of course, before he surrendered in excess of 50,000 British and Commonwealth troops to 30,000 or so Japanese, and thus condemned my father-in-law, with many others, to the building of the notorious Burma railway. My father-in-law survived – nearly four out of five did not. Incompetence from senior military officers is, unfortunately, perfectly believable – and so too is the inevitable consequence of not being properly prepared for war. Tacitus, in the *Annals*:

> *Then a native horde surrounded them. When all else had been ravaged or burnt, the garrison concentrated itself in the temple. After two days' siege, it fell to storm.*

And when it did, compared to the way those conquering Britons of AD60 behaved, the 20th-century Japanese probably acted like angels.

Dio follows Boudicca's long-winded speech to her Iceni army by merely saying that she led '... her army against the Romans ... to sack and plunder two Roman cities, and, as I have said, to wreak indescribable slaughter ...' But he then goes on to describe that slaughter all too well. Those who do not suffer from weak stomachs or nightmares may read it at their leisure, in the Appendix.

Was the garrison which concentrated in the temple the small one mentioned as being on the spot, plus Decianus's 200 and the old people and women who had not been evacuated? Had the several thousand tough, experienced, well-armed ex-legionary veterans really hopped it (undertaken a strategic retreat, I mean)? A comment earlier in the *Agricola* said that 'Veterans were butchered, colonies burned to the ground ...' So perhaps they were all butchered or died fighting. But if that were the case one would have expected an account of a heroic and really hard-fought battle against overwhelming odds, and what we have just read certainly is not one of those. Perhaps some of the veterans stayed in the colony to be massacred, and others didn't. Perhaps the ones who were butchered were the ones who were elderly, sick or infirm and couldn't march away, or were those who had stayed out too long in their country farms and had been caught by rebel raiding parties.

There is a quotation from Dio which might help shed a light on this question. It comes later on, in his account of Suetonius's speech before the big battle:

> Neither fear them because they have burned a couple of cities; for they did not capture them by force nor after a battle, but one was betrayed and the other abandoned to them.

We learn later that Verulamium was abandoned, and Londinium, of course, was a place for common traders, and didn't count as a city and even if it did, it was still abandoned. So it must have been Camulodunum that was betrayed.

Betrayed is a pretty emotive word. If some three thousand veteran soldiers had marched away from an apparently indefensible city, intending to live and fight another day, were they cowards, or was that militarily the right thing to do? The governor, Suetonius himself, abandoned Verulamium and Londinium for the good enough reason that both were indefensible, without being accused of lacking moral fibre.

Tacitus only hints strongly that something was not quite right at Camulodunum. Dio seems positive that something was wrong, but for some reason or other they were both reluctant to come out and say just what. Perhaps what really happened would have embarrassed a Roman audience, or maybe the relatives of Camulodunum's commanding officer were still very important people in Rome at the time, and so the matter was hushed up. We are left to speculate.

There is another very important question that now needs to be considered before we can let Tacitus carry on with his story, and that is, just who were these rebels who sacked Camulodunum? Both of our sources generally refer to Queen Boudicca's Iceni army with a hint of respect, yet here Tacitus is talking rather scornfully of a 'native horde' storming the city. Are they one and the same military force?

It is much too easy to assume that Tacitus's words are telling us that the Iceni army had marched all the way from Norfolk just to take vengeance on the Romans for their ill-treatment of the Trinovantes. But Tacitus's words do not actually say that is what happened, and since we have already questioned whether the Iceni would have 'particularly hated' the Roman settlers as much as the Trinovantes did, so too should we question another assumption that doesn't sound quite right.

Frankly, one would have thought that the Iceni, with a national rebellion to organise and promote, had far more lofty and important things on their minds at that point in time – like ensuring their own survival. The suggestion has already been made that the Camulodunum colonists would probably never have been allowed to interfere directly in the affairs of the favoured client kingdom, which anyway was some considerable distance to the north. So why, having taken the monumental decision to rebel, would the Iceni have ignored their own self interests and marched away from their lands, leaving them and their wives and their families undefended and open to attack by Roman troops – when there were so many Roman troops about? There were more than 6,000 of them near Lincoln – a whole legion plus auxiliaries – only a couple of days' march away from the Iceni homelands. The IXth legion posed a vastly more serious threat to the Iceni rebels than ever the 3,000-odd veterans, who were anyway not a mobile force and only there to defend Camulodunum, would have done.

Is it not more likely that this 'native horde' consisted only of local Trinovantes tribesmen, who having learned of the Iceni rebellion, were encouraged to rebel themselves, but were fighting, at that point in time, quite independently of the Iceni? If they were more of a rabble than a disciplined force, that would be perfectly understandable. The Trinovantes were not the active and organised tribe they may once have been. They had been subservient to the Catuvellauni long before the coming of the Romans, and that had been followed by seventeen years of a dominating Roman presence. So it would not be at all surprising if bands of rebels from the Camulodunum area acted initially like a rabble, with vengeance and retaliation against the Romans primarily in their minds. Naturally they would have avoided the well manned forts and out-posts and attacked the easy loot-rich farms and villas first, but if there are enough of them, even rabbles and mobs can overwhelm larger places that are not adequately defended – and Camulodunum certainly seems to have fitted that description.

Tacitus himself may shed a light on the question of whether there might have been more than one rebel force active in eastern England at that point in time. In the *Agricola* he summarises the whole rebellion all too briefly:

> . . . *the whole island rose under the leadership of Boudicca, a lady of royal descent – for Britons make no distinction of sex in their leaders. They hunted down the Roman troops in their scattered posts, stormed the forts and assaulted the colony itself, in which they saw their slavery focused; nor did the angry victors deny themselves any form of savage cruelty.*

Then he adds this in his *Annals*:

The natives enjoyed plundering and thought of nothing else. Bypassing forts and garrisons, they made for where loot was richest and protection weakest.

Now, Tacitus cannot have it both ways. Either the rebels stormed the forts and the garrisons, or they didn't. Unless, of course, Tacitus was describing the behaviour of two different forces, one an untrained, ad hoc collection of disaffected individuals who were consumed with an overwhelming hatred of all things Romans, and the other an army which was purposeful, disciplined and capable of storming forts.

Tacitus then goes on to give further evidence to support the suggestion that there was indeed a rebel army in eastern England which was sufficiently disciplined and well led to be able to storm forts. He follows his account of the fall of Camulodunum by stating in his *Annals* that:

The ninth Roman division, commanded by Quintus Petilius Cerialis Caesius Rufus, attempted to relieve the town, but was stopped by the victorious Britons and routed. Its entire infantry force was massacred, while the commander escaped to his camp with his cavalry and sheltered behind its defences.

There is no mention here of forts and outposts, but there can surely be no doubt that the rebel troops who took on the infantry from the ninth division, and massacred them, must have been well led and disciplined, and who else could they have been but Boudicca's Iceni army?

It is therefore quite possible, indeed it is very probable, that there were at least two active rebel forces of reasonable size operating independently in eastern England at that time, which were, presumably, intending at some stage to meet somewhere and combine into a larger army. There is also evidence, which Tacitus has yet to relate, which suggests that there might well have been another sizeable independent rebel force in the West Country. None of this should really surprise us though. It is surely to be expected that any tribe joining the rebellion would have first mobilised its forces under their own tribal leaders, and only have set off to join up with the main group after they had pillaged and ravaged any easily overwhelmed local Roman targets. In fact there were probably dozens of small rebel bands wandering about looking for loot or Romans to slaughter, or simply on their way to join up with the main armies.

It was an age with no methods of mass communication, so to assume that all the rebels in the extensive area of East Anglia and the East Midlands had somehow managed to combine into a single military entity at that early stage in the rebellion must surely be an illogical interpretation of Tacitus's words. Which means, of course, that the Iceni army may never have marched south to Camulodunum, because the Trinovantes, if they were indeed Tacitus's 'native horde', might well have stormed and sacked the inadequately defended city on their own.

That is an important point to keep in mind, because Tacitus's words about the defeat of the IXth legion have thrown up yet another easily made assumption that, on the face of it, does not really make good sense. Let us read Tacitus's words about the battle with the IXth legion once again. The legion commander's name is given in full, because he too turns out to have been a future governor of Britain.

> The ninth Roman division, commanded by Quintus Petilius Cerialis Caesius Rufus, attempted to relieve the town, but was stopped by the victorious Britons and routed. Its entire infantry force was massacred, while the commander escaped to his camp with his cavalry and sheltered behind its defences.

The first part of this passage is generally accepted by historians as meaning that the IXth legion set out to relieve Camulodunum, but were attacked and routed on the way by the same victorious Britons who had stormed the city.

But why would the IXth legion have been going to Camulodunum? One would have thought that as soon as they had learned of the Iceni rebellion, their very first action would have been to march to the Iceni capital where the trouble had started, and put down the uprising before it could spread. That is what one would have expected them to do, and if what is suggested is not what we would expect, then surely we are right to be suspicious.

If Cerialis was really setting out for Camulodunum rather than to the Iceni's capital, then the only sensible reason must be that he learned of the 'native horde' threat to the city before he had learned that the Iceni were rebelling.

Could news of the rebellion have travelled from Norfolk to Camulodunum, and then back up to Lincoln – a distance of some 200 miles, more quickly than the same news had travelled from Norfolk to Lincoln? The approximate distances for messages to travel are, very roughly: Iceni to Lincoln 30–40 miles; Camulodunum to Lincoln 110–120 miles. That might help put things into perspective.

It would surely have taken a couple of days or so for the news of the Iceni rebellion to have travelled the 80 odd miles to the Trinovantes in Essex. Then several more days must have elapsed before the 'native horde' was mobilised in sufficient numbers to be able to surround the city. That mobilisation may, of course, have coincided with the period between the Roman request for Decianus's help and the arrival of his 200 ill-armed reinforcements. Tacitus does not tell us that a similar request for help was also made to the IXth legion, but if such a message had been sent from Camulodunum on the 120-mile journey through territory, which by then was probably seething with armed rebels, that would probably have taken another two or three days to get to Lincoln. So, it would have needed at least a week, most probably much longer, for the news of the rebellion to have reached Cerialis by that circuitous route.

Whereas Cerialis may have learned of the revolt directly from Norfolk by a mounted courier in less than a day. Even if there was no such courier we should bear in mind that as soon as the Iceni rebelled, the movement of normal Roman domestic traffic through Iceni territory would have immediately ceased – in both directions. If Cerialis did not learn of the rebellion directly, the interruption of Roman com-munications would soon have alerted him to trouble, and scouts would have been sent to find out what was going on. Even on that basis it seems perfectly reasonable to assume that Cerialis would certainly have known of the Iceni rebellion several days before he learned there was anything amiss in Camulodunum.

So would Cerialis have ignored the news of the Iceni revolt, and only acted when he had received a message from Camulodunum? That is surely very unlikely, but it would be very interesting to read the answers to that question from those historians who put forward the simplistic view that Cerialis and the IXth legion did leave the Iceni lands unthreatened, and proceeded to march down to Camulodunum. That proposition is rather like saying that if riots were reported in Trafalgar Square on a Saturday night, the Metropolitan Police Commissioner would do nothing until the following Friday, and then think he could solve the first problem by sending his riot squads to a different trouble spot.

It might just be possible that Cerialis did nothing until he had received direct orders from Suetonius, who was, of course, a long way away, but that too seems very unlikely. It was Cerialis's job to deal with localised trouble. He shouldn't have needed telling, and besides, Tacitus later refers to 'the price only too clearly paid by the divisional commander's rashness'. If Suetonius thought that Cerialis's actions were rash, then it is unlikely that the IXth legion's commander was carrying out his direct orders. Almost certainly Cerialis was acting *rashly* on his own initiative, and since *rashly* is hardly the word to use to describe someone who is being inactive and dilatory, we ought to come back to square one, and assume that he hadn't been idle. The failure to take prompt military action when he first heard of the Iceni rebellion would surely have brought far more serious accusations on his head than mere rashness.

There is something else in Tacitus's words that might also be significant in this respect. He actually says that the IXth legion set out to relieve the 'town'. But Tacitus is pretty hot on what was a town or a city. London wasn't a city remember – Verulamium and Camulodunum were, and if he doesn't refer to the latter place as a city, then he calls it the colony. On that basis the 'town' Tacitus says the IXth legion were setting out to relieve ought, in fact, not to have been Camulodunum anyway. If that is so, then where might the IXth have been going? The logical and most sensible answer still has to be – to the Iceni lands where the rebellion started. So it would not be unreasonable to tentatively suggest that the 'town' Tacitus refers to may have been the Iceni tribal capital – wherever that was. Perhaps in that place there was a small garrisoned fort or outpost in which Decianus's men took shelter, and which was, or had once been, under siege.

There is another point which might or might not be relevant. Peddars Way not only leads directly from Lincoln into the Iceni tribal area – it then goes straight on to Camulodunum. So, if it wasn't for that use of the word 'town', we might have assumed that Tacitus simply looked at his map, found that Peddars Way led to Camulodunum, and erroneously deduced that the Roman capital was Cerialis's destination.

Some of Tacitus's words in the last few passages quoted seem to lack a certain amount of clarity. The reason for that may be quite simple. He obviously used several different sources for his account of these events, because no one observer could have been everywhere at the same time and seen everything. The first of his sources, perhaps Agricola himself, certainly seems to have been with Suetonius in Anglesey. The next may possibly have been one of Decianus's tax collectors, who gave a perhaps censored account of what had really happened at the Iceni capital after Prasutagus's death. Another may have been a Roman who had served with the IXth legion and knew of Boudicca's army, and a fourth had perhaps been in Camulodunum or Londinium, and had seen the 'native hordes'.

Combining all those different viewpoints of what was happening in different places at different times into a single continuous narrative would not have been easy. In fact Tacitus was not able to do it. He has already had to break off from his Anglesey source, and will return to it later. He may have told the stories from the other sources separately too, but without giving us a clearly defined gap between them. After the Anglesey story comes the account of the tax collectors at the Iceni capital. Next is the storming of Camulodunum, with its Trinovantes or local colonist viewpoint, and after that we have the story of the massacre of the IXth legion. That may explain why Camulodunum suddenly seemed to have become the core of the rebellion, and why Tacitus did not realise he was contradicting himself about the storming of forts – and also why the battle between the Iceni and the IXth legion seems to be out of chronological sequence, because logically that ought to have happened before Camulodunum was stormed, not after.

Unfortunately for us neither Dio nor Tacitus seem to have had a really good reporting source from within the Iceni and the other rebel parties to help put things into perspective. As a result we have learned little or nothing about what the Iceni did, or set out to do, in order to make their rebellion into a widespread uprising.

To fill that major gap, and perhaps give ourselves a more balanced view of what was going on, we must try to put ourselves into Queen Boudicca's, and the other rebel leaders' minds, and hopefully reason as they may have done.

CHAPTER X

Queen Boudicca's Military Options

Tacitus and Dio are both adamant that Boudicca was the leader of the rebellion, so we can reasonably assume that she promptly took over all the powers and authority of her husband when he died. In fact, if Prasutagus had been sick or incapacitated for any length of time before his death, she may have effectively been running the affairs of the Iceni kingdom anyway.

When matters had reached the crisis point for the Iceni, the first thing Queen Boudicca probably did was to call a meeting of all those officials and advisers who would have made up Prasutagus's court or executive cabinet. She would have needed their wholehearted agreement and backing. Then the discussion would have turned to the subject of how to make their localised rebellion into a successful national one.

The first decision made would have been acted upon promptly, and that would probably have been to call for the immediate mobilisation of all those Iceni males capable of bearing arms, although the very youngest and the oldest may only have been used as garrisons, escorts, or generally for home defence. The same thing might well have been set in motion in the neighbouring Lincolnshire tribe of the Coritani, if Prasutagus had had any special influence over them.

The war committee's next task would probably have been the wording of a message which would be sent to all the other tribal chiefs in Britain, informing them of the Iceni rebellion, and exhorting them also to rise up against the Roman administration. However, the message would probably not have been quite as simple as that. Once their couriers had mounted and ridden off into the distance, they couldn't be called back to add a *postscriptum*. So those messages would also have needed to contain the outline of a viable plan, which, provided all those who rebelled pulled in the same direction and co-operated, might result in the destruction of the Roman forces.

What might such a hastily contrived plan have consisted of? Perhaps each tribal chief would have been urged to use the first of his mobilised forces to besiege and isolate each Roman fort or outpost in or near his tribal area. When that was done, any surplus rebel troops should be sent to a particular rendezvous, where they would eventually meet up with the British national field army which was gathering somewhere under Queen Boudicca's command. The allied army would then, when it was strong enough, hunt down and defeat whatever mobile forces the Romans still had left in Britain. After that, Queen Boudicca's victorious troops would go round the country and destroy each of the remaining besieged Roman forts one by one. Then all Britain would be free.

That is a very simple plan, but then, a good plan should be simple, and we would be very patronising if we thought that the British of two thousand years ago could not have conceived such a thing, or even worse – that they had no plan at all.

Those messages would have needed some sort of official seal of authority, if there was such a thing. Possibly none of the messages would have been taken seriously if they had been simply verbal, unless the courier was someone who was already known and trusted. Perhaps the Druids had a part to play in that respect. Particular care would have been necessary when communicating with King Cogidumnus down on the south coast, and Venutius, or whoever was then leader of the Brigantes. The support of those two, who could raise large numbers of troops, would have seemed vital to the Iceni, but then, so too would the co-operation of the Silures and the Ordovices in Wales, and the Dobunni and the Durotriges in the West Country. To make that simple outline plan work, those last four tribes would have needed to blockade all the forts and outposts of the IInd legion, the XXth, and the XIVth.

Having said that, all of a sudden the chances of the Iceni triggering a successful national revolt do not sound quite so good. With the exception of Cogidumnus, and perhaps the Brigantes, it is highly unlikely that any of those Welsh or West Country tribal leaders had ever received so-called gifts from the Emperor Claudius, and neither is it likely that Seneca had loaned them any sesterces, so Decianus would not have been causing them grief and anguish with his debt collection tactics. A common hatred of the Romans would have been the only sentiment the Iceni could have appealed to, and that would have sounded a bit thin coming from a tribe that had been happily co-operating with the enemy for seventeen years. The other problem the Iceni might have had was knowing just who were the current tribal leaders in far off Wales and Devon, and when their messengers finally arrived, would those tribes even know that there ever had been a King Prasutagus in that distant and remote part of Britain we now call Norfolk, let alone that his surviving Queen was named Boudicca? Divide and rule was certainly a Roman policy, so it is unlikely that they ever allowed the British kings and chiefs to socialise, meet up occasionally, and get to know each other well.

This is all speculation. Should we be indulging in such flights of fancy? Well, we are trying to fill in a huge gap left by our sources, and there is nothing wrong with reasoned speculation, provided one doesn't then draw firm conclusions from it. Useful lessons are sometimes learned from experimental archaeology, so we too might gain understanding from some experimental history.

That outline plan was simple enough – one hardly needs a degree in military tactics to come up with that, but is it likely that such a thing was ever mooted? Tacitus says that 'armies were isolated', and we will find out later that the IInd legion near Exeter would get bottled up. So too would the remnants of the IXth legion, and the first job that the 'native horde' did down at Camulodunum was to surround the place. Possibly those are instances of that, or a similar plan being implemented.

If Boudicca and her Iceni council did have such a plan, would they have been capable of organising an effective army to support it? If our surmises on the responsibilities of client kings are anywhere near correct, then the answer must surely be yes. The Iceni court or council would have been made up of intelligent experienced people, who could administer the affairs, and maintain the peace in a large, populous, and reputedly wealthy territory, certainly well enough to satisfy their own direct ruler, and presumably the Roman authorities as well. There would have been treasurers and accountants, police chiefs, Druid lawyers and academics perhaps, as well as an aristocracy who probably concentrated on the martial arts.

Having signed and sealed all those messages to the other British tribal leaders, and seen their couriers off and on their way, Boudicca and her council would probably have then sat down to chew over the next, and this time absolutely vital question – what were they going to do about all those Romans troops of the IXth legion, who were less than two days' march away near Lincoln?

Surely there would have been nothing more certain in Boudicca's, and her advisors' minds, than the fact that as soon as the IXth learned of the Iceni revolt they would immediately send a strong force with the intention of nipping the rebellion in the bud, before it could spread. That was the IXth's specific function – to deal with incursions and rebellions in the east of Britain. That was why it was where it was. The legion may have had a good proportion of its numbers out manning six or seven forts and outposts on the Trent, but those left in their base camp would still be enough to provide a sizeable task force.

Unfortunately we have no idea of the real time scale between action and reaction, but it would probably not have taken very long for the news of the Iceni's rebellion to reach Lincoln. Possibly Decianus's debt collection officers managed to send a mounted messenger to the legion's commander with a plea for help, before succumbing to the Iceni's wrath.

That commander's first reaction may have been to send a message of his own to Suetonius in Anglesey, just to tell him what was going on, but then he would almost certainly have given orders for an adequate strike force of infantry and cavalry to get themselves ready to march. The IXth might even have been on the road to the Iceni within twenty-four hours of the actual rebellion breaking out. So the Iceni council would not have had much time to prepare a force to meet and confront them. If the Romans turned up and caught the Iceni half mobilised and in confusion, the slaughter would be great and the rebellion over before it had really started.

We have assumed that Prasutagus would have had some sort of police force with which to keep order in his lands. That, and the first batches of armed warriors to turn up might have been sent out to meet the advancing Romans.

Tacitus has already told us what happened when they met – the Britons were victorious. But there is more to this battle than just the winning of it. It confirms the assumption that Boudicca and her staff were able to make sensible and successful military decisions. Those two forces would never have met by chance. They must have been looking for each other, and it is most likely that the winner had the initiative, either of surprise, or the choosing of the battleground, or both.

We have already discussed Norfolk's Roman roads at some length, and this battle with the IXth legion is really the reason why. I am assuming, not unexpectedly I'm sure, that most probably the IXth legion would have been marching southwards on the road called Peddars Way, which leads directly to where they needed to go to put the rebellion down – right into the heart of Iceni country. We can discuss possible alternative routes later.

Perhaps the warlike Iceni had been playing war games during the years of peace, and already had an ambush plan in mind for just such a contingency. Perhaps the IXth legion was caught unawares while crossing the Metaris Estuary, in much the same way as Duke William of Normandy, a thousand years later, caught the French as they tried to cross the Dives. Perhaps Cerialis merely walked into a simple ambush on the road. He certainly did something that was rash and most likely foolhardy, but precisely what that was is something we will, unfortunately, probably never know.

The Iceni, however, certainly seem to have forecast Roman reactions correctly, and made the right moves to counter them. Having gathered together their nearest armed levies, they clearly had not marched south to sack Camulodunum nor to exact petty vengeance for the ill-treatment of the Trinovantes – both of which in this context now seem rather ludicrous suggestions. They had gone looking for Cerialis and his IXth legion instead – and when they had found them, they had massacred the Roman infantry.

What happened to the rest of the IXth legion's task force? Tacitus told us that the commander '. . . escaped to his camp with his cavalry and sheltered behind its defences'. What does the word 'camp' mean in this context?

When on the march the Romans would camp for the night behind temporary defences that would be proof against a surprise attack, but those defences were probably dismantled before marching on next morning, to prevent them being used by unauthorised forces. If Cerialis and his cavalry had merely escaped back to their last night's stopping place, then there ought not to have been any defences still standing, and even if there were, without their infantry their numbers would have been clearly insufficient to defend the place adequately.

We also use the word 'camp' to describe a permanent military base with a garrison. Cerialis's permanent military base was near Lincoln, and that was surely the only place with adequate defences behind which he could find shelter. So, having massacred his infantry, the surviving Iceni forces must have chased Cerialis and his cavalry right back to his legion's base camp in Lincoln. That is not speculation. That is what Tacitus's words tell us. What other sensible meaning can they have?

Rather than ever going south to Camulodunum, that first hastily gathered group of Iceni warriors must surely have ended up besieging Cerialis in his base camp near Lincoln. They must have been there quickly and in reasonable numbers too, or else Cerialis would have been off like a shot to gather together all the garrisons of his other forts and outposts. They would have given him a powerful force of at least 4,000 troops, with which he could either have gone back to attack the Iceni, or have marched off to join Suetonius's army, but we will find out from Tacitus that he did neither. The Iceni obviously had him bottled up, and kept him that way.

Those legionaries who had been massacred probably only numbered about 2,000, which is the figure that Tacitus later tells us were needed to bring the legion back to full strength, but there would also have been auxiliaries involved, who might or might not be included in that figure. No doubt the Iceni victors would have made good use of the 2,000 sets of Roman infantry arms and armour.

For that number of experienced troops to be annihilated in anything like a normal battle, the rebels' casualties too must surely have been considerable. They may have included the Iceni's best leaders and their bravest warriors, who would naturally have been in the forefront of any fighting.

Before we move on we must dutifully consider the alternative routes on which the IXth legion might have marched to their battle with the Iceni. Those authorities who ignore the existence of Peddars Way, and that is all of them as far as I am aware, and who are yet happy to accept that the IXth was based in Lincolnshire, hold that the legion marched down Ermine Street, turned left at Huntingdon, and were massacred somewhere on the Via Devana near Cambridge. However, they are not only assuming that

Ermine Street actually existed that far north at that time, which is itself a dubious proposition, but also that the IXth legion was on its way to Camulodunum, and we've already considered that confused possibility in some depth.

Others, who prefer to think that the IXth legion was based miles away from their outposts on the Trent, at Longthorpe near Peterborough, have them travelling on a road that goes south-east from that place towards Camulodunum, but Margary, the foremost authority on Roman roads in Britain, states that a coin of the Emperor Trajan was found in the footings of that particular road, so it would not have been constructed until after the late 90s AD, at the very earliest.

Let us get back to Queen Boudicca, who was presumably now with her staff and troops at Lincoln. On the face of it, they had achieved their first main objective, to defeat the IXth legion's strike force, but the legionaries in the other forts and outposts along the frontier would also need to be blockaded. To do that Boudicca would have had to detach well in excess of 4,000 warriors from her small army just to contain them, and even more if her intention was for those forts to be stormed.

But there was a new danger which now needed to be added to all her other concerns and worries. Lincoln was on the Fosse Way, and Boudicca and her advisors would surely have known why the Fosse Way had been built. It was to enable the Roman legions to provide rapid support for each other in moments of crisis. She would not have a clear picture of what was going on in the rest of England or what other dangers now threatened, but as far as she was probably concerned, at any moment a Roman force from the IInd, XIVth and the XXth legions, or even Suetonius with all his Anglesey army, might suddenly come charging along that road to relieve the besieged IXth legion.

So a new and much larger Iceni army would therefore have been needed to block the Fosse Way and confront that potential danger, but until significant reinforcements arrived, Boudicca could have done little more than just bite her finger nails, if such bad habits existed in those days, and send scouting parties west along the Fosse Way to locate the nearest Roman troops, find out what they were up to, and to give as much warning as possible of any approaching threat.

In the meantime, the Iceni would have wanted to storm all the IXth legion's forts and slaughter their garrisons, then none of their forces would have needed to be tied down in static sieges. We know from Tacitus in the *Agricola* that some forts and outposts were stormed, and it may be that the ones he refers to were those of the IXth legion, but attackers of well fortified positions, where the defenders are alert and fighting for their lives, are always at a disadvantage. If the Iceni tried it, then their casualties would almost certainly have been high, perhaps many times higher than those of the defenders. So the storming of forts might actually have turned out to be a drain on resources rather than freeing them up. Perhaps having learned that lesson the hard way, further attempts were abandoned.

Boudicca's messages to other tribes would have taken time to be delivered, and even longer for their councils of war to meet and make decisions – and much longer still for warrior groups to muster and march to a rendezvous. Those response times may have been weeks rather than days, for all we know.

However, reinforcements from the already mobilised Iceni homelands would certainly have been hurrying in, and bands from the nearest tribes that had also decided to rebel might be turning up, impatient and eager to get on with the fight.

So all those problems connected with the concentration of a large, mainly static military force would have started to rear their ugly heads. Some of those on Boudicca's staff would have to sort out food supplies and wagons to move them, and fodder for cavalry horses and draught animals. Accommodation or camping space would need to be allocated, and weapons found, made or improvised. Officers needed to be appointed and a command structure set up, and measures put in place to maintain discipline. Tribesmen who for generations had been at odds with each other might combine in a common potentially loot-rich cause, but that would not have made them good bed-fellows. There would have been minor councils of war, with some chiefs wanting to attack south, west or north, others proposing a defensive 'wait and see' strategy, and some merely wanting the chance to get some booty. Those councils could easily have become forums of dissent and rancour rather than of constructive policies or ideas. In the meantime, the area in which the army was collecting would soon have become ravaged and denuded of supplies.

Boudicca and the top Iceni war council would have been anxious to get the army moving, just as soon as it had expanded to the size which would enable them to meet Suetonius's legionaries head on with a certainty of success. But how big should that be? That would be another difficult decision for Boudicca and her colleagues to make. To have fought a battle while still weak in numbers would have been to risk defeat and utter disaster, so they may have contented themselves, while reinforcements were still arriving, with simply ensuring that the rest of the IXth legion did not join up with the main Roman army. No doubt Boudicca's scouts had eventually located the governor and his troops, and knew just what he was up to, because by then Suetonius would almost certainly have been on the move.

If you still feel it is somehow possible that the Iceni did go south in strength to Camulodunum, rather than north to Lincoln, then you must ask yourself which other rebel army was large enough to block the Fosse Way, and at the same time besiege the forts on the Trent, because there must have been one – otherwise Suetonius the governor would have collected what was nigh on 4,000, or even more, of his IXth legion, and we know, or we will know, because Tacitus will tell us later on, that he didn't.

What else might have been going on in Britain at this time? Well, although Cerialis was now blockaded, he may have found the means to send out messages to Suetonius, Decianus and others, explaining what had happened, and asking for immediate assistance. It would not be surprising if, in those messages, he tended to overstate the strength and extent of the revolt, to explain or excuse his defeat.

In the *Annals*, Tacitus tersely states the effect that such a message may have had on Decianus.

> *The imperial agent Catus Decianus, horrified by the catastrophe and by his unpopularity, withdrew to Gaul. It was his rapacity which had driven the province to war.*

With the east of Britain seething with rebel groups ready to lynch any Roman on sight, official messages and messengers would almost certainly have been delayed or even lost completely. News would not arrive in a neat chronological order, so the word 'catastrophe' may refer to Cerialis's defeat, or the storming of Camulodunum, or both, but it doesn't matter – Decianus scarpered. Possibly he also sent a message to Suetonius before leaving, saying something on the lines of: 'Everything was lost – all the eastern tribes were in violent revolt – and at a great risk to his own life and limb – he was bravely taking the province's petty cash box and treasury to Gaul, to prevent it falling into rebel hands.' If he did so, it obviously cut no ice with Tacitus, who we know was a Suetonius supporter, and so the blame was laid firmly on Decianus's shoulders: 'It was his rapacity which had driven the province to war.' With the hindsight of nearly two thousand years, it really is difficult to disagree.

That tidies up both Tacitus's and Dio's accounts of the rebellion so far, and we have also just about exhausted our examination of the Iceni's various logical strategic and tactical options. If this exercise has resulted in the overall perspective of the rebellion being widened to include an otherwise missing British viewpoint, then it has achieved its purpose. The participants on both sides would have been intelligent people trying to act sensibly, while under great mental and nervous stress and probably scared almost out of their wits because of the danger they all found themselves in.

It is time for Tacitus and Dio to carry on with their story, and for us to return to Anglesey, to find out how the Roman governor, Suetonius Paulinus, reacted to the news of the catastrophe.

CHAPTER XI
The Roman Governor's Reactions

Tacitus's narrative now returns to the Roman army which had just successfully invaded Anglesey. The imperial governor, Gaius Suetonius Paulinus, had learned of a sudden rebellion in the south-east of his province.

Firstly, there may have been a message from the IXth legion, reporting that Decianus's officials had had trouble with the Iceni. That probably did not disturb the governor's sleep a great deal, since he would have known that Decianus was collecting debts and resorting to severe measures.

The order of subsequent messages would have depended on how disrupted the Roman cross-country courier service was at that time – but the next one, if Cerialis had been able to dispatch it before being besieged in his camp, should have told him of the defeat of the IXth legion's detachment. That may shortly have been followed by a dispatch from Decianus, saying, perhaps, that all the eastern tribes were in revolt, Camulodunum was under siege, or that it had been stormed – and that Cerialis's attempt to put down the rebellion had failed miserably, and that he was bravely doing a runner to Gaul.

For Suetonius that would have been devastating news. His province, which only a few days before had seemed so safe and settled, had started to disintegrate. Bloody battles would have to be fought to restore order, if indeed that was still possible, and if he didn't win them, he might well lose his life when he faced the wrath of Nero. At best he faced humiliation and the scorn of his peers.

In Anglesey he was miles from anywhere and effectively isolated. In fact, if the rebels got themselves organised quickly, he was in danger of being completely cut off from the rest of the province. If he didn't get a grip on affairs pretty smartly, he might soon find himself cowering behind a hastily built stockade, running short of supplies, and waiting for the final rush of native warriors to signal his humiliating defeat. That may sound rather over dramatised, but surely such thoughts and emotions would have been in the back of Suetonius's mind as he grappled with the need to make sensible decisions.

We know that Suetonius reacted quickly, so what did he do next? Our school history books tell us that the governor simply got on his horse, left his army to follow on behind, and rode with a cavalry escort down to Londinium, in order, it is said, that he could see the situation for himself. That is very unlikely. He was far too exulted a person to go off doing the reconnaissance and intelligence gathering work of a junior officer. To illustrate just how powerful and important Suetonius was, Rome had only about twenty-five legions in the whole of its empire at the time, and Suetonius was the commander-in-chief of four of them. He was also one of only twenty or so provincial Roman governors. In the list of the VIPs of the time Suetonius must have come somewhere in the top dozen or so. There would have been a sizeable staff of senior officers about him, including, possibly, the commanders of the XXth, XIVth, and IInd legions, and even the young Agricola, among many other *aides de camp*. If he wanted reconnaissance patrols out, and he most surely would have, there would have been plenty of fit, young and experienced officers eager to undertake them. Those reconnaissance patrols would have needed to penetrate deeply into hostile areas, and would have been in constant danger of attack or ambush. It was certainly not a job for a middle-aged governor-general. Would Montgomery, after El Alamein, have said to his junior generals that he was going off on his own to find out what Rommel was up to? The Duke of Wellington certainly wouldn't have left his army in the care of any of his subordinate generals from choice. If he wasn't there in person, he said many times in so many words, something usually went wrong.

Suetonius may only have had about five or six thousand legionaries and auxiliaries with him at the time, but that was still the strongest and most powerful Roman force in Britain. If the rebellion was to be stamped out, that army would need to be very skilfully handled – by its commander-in-chief.

There is another point to bear in mind. If the most important man in Britain had gone off to do the work of a junior lieutenant, and his army had been attacked and defeated while he was heading towards safety in Gaul, he would have been accused of desertion and cowardice – with some justification too. That would be like actually asking Nero for a phial of imperial poison. So, probably, like Mary's little lamb, only not quite so meek, wherever Suetonius went, his army was sure to go too.

Where did the notion that Suetonius might have acted in such an unprofessional manner come from? It did not come from Tacitus. In the *Annals* he states:

> But Suetonius, undismayed, marched through disaffected territory to Londinium.

That is surely clear enough, unless one is so pedantic as to insist that those words mean he marched on his own. Wellington marched, Napoleon marched, unfortunately Rommel usually advanced, but we know they didn't go on their own. It would be unreasonable to interpret Tacitus's words in any other way. The 'undismayed', is probably merely to tell us that Suetonius wasn't in a panic, or at least not much of one.

Why is the idea that Suetonius left his army behind thus propounded? The reason may be, even though there is no evidence from our sources to support it, that the decisive battle between the Romans and the rebels is deemed by many historians to have taken place somewhere in the East Midlands. If Suetonius had marched his army down to Londinium, for the battle to have subsequently been fought in the East Midlands, he would have had to march his troops all the way back north again. Which doesn't make sense. So, to make the circumstances fit the story, it seems to have been decreed that Suetonius must have left his army behind, and rejoined them later – after he'd been to Londinium – but that makes even less sense.

Let us move on, hopefully with reasonably open minds, and discuss Suetonius's other options. He could not stay where he was. He needed to cross the Welsh mountains which were isolating him from his province, and then the only way he could sensibly have gone was south.

If he moved quickly, before the rebels were able to amass an army large enough to block his way, he and his legionaries ought to be able to fight their way through the Midlands and down to the Thames crossing. If things looked really hopeless when he got there, he could then have carried on to the south coast, where they could all have disembarked for Gaul. But that would have been his worst case scenario – his very last resort – because it would mean abandoning his province and leaving the rest of his widely scattered legionaries to be massacred, if they could not also fight their way out.

South of the Thames, however, were the lands ruled by the client king Cogidumnus, whom Suetonius had probably met several times during the past two years, and may, in fact, have got to know reasonably well. It was probably the most stable and most romanised area in the whole of the province. If the king was still loyal and more importantly, was still in control of his tribes, then Suetonius might have the chance to gather some of his widely scattered troops, and using the king's territory as a supply base, he might then be able to set about taking the offensive and start quelling the revolt.

So, his options would have seem simple enough, to stay and risk being surrounded and annihilated, or to hurry south to Londinium. Tacitus tells us that Suetonius did go south to Londinium, and both he and Dio say that he moved fast.

However, before he left Anglesey, Suetonius would surely have done at least two things. Firstly, he would not have wanted to abandon those of his troops injured in the Mona battle, but if he took them with him, they might slow his march – so, possibly, he would have arranged for them to be evacuated by sea in the ships of his supporting navy.

Secondly, he would most likely have sent urgent messages to all his outlying forts and garrisons on the Welsh borders, and down in Devon and Dorset, and also probably to Cerialis's outposts on the Trent, telling them what he intended to do, and that they should also attempt to fight their way south.

Suetonius's quickest route to Cogidumnus's territory, once clear of the Welsh mountains, would have been down Watling Street, via Verulamium, to the Thames crossing at Londinium.

Some authorities claim that Suetonius would not have crossed the mountains, but would have marched the longer distance round the coast to Chester and then on down to Wroxeter, and so he might, if that was the quickest route. There would certainly have been no Roman road along the coast then, and Chester, if it existed at that time, would have only been a minor frontier outpost. The city was probably not built until Anglesey and North Wales were finally brought under Roman control, which may have been after AD77, because the name Cn. Julius Agricola is impressed into a piece of lead piping found there

Once they were on Watling Street, a road built specifically to enable troops to move quickly from one place to another, the Roman legionaries should have been able to put their best foot forward, and make good speed.

There were three places on Watling Street where rebels coming from the east on roads or tracks could have cut Suetonius off from the south. The first of those we have already mentioned, namely the junction with the Fosse Way. The second would be where the Icknield Way from Norfolk crossed Watling Street some miles north of Verulamium, and the third would be the Thames crossing itself, at Londinium.

Now we need to ask again the question we left unanswered in the last chapter. Why, when he came to the Fosse Way junction, did Suetonius not turn left and collect what remained of the IXth legion? They were only thirty or forty miles from Watling Street – less than two days' march. If he had sent them messages ordering them to fight their way out and join him, they obviously did not, or could not, obey him.

So, had Suetonius's scouts told him that the rebel forces blocking the Fosse Way were too strong for his small Roman army? Had Boudicca's scouts told her, at the same time, that her rebel army was not yet strong enough to tackle the Roman legionaries?

That might have been a moment of amusingly confused non-confrontation, had not the decisions made on either side been of such a magnitude that they may have significantly affected the outcome of the war. The net result seems to have been that the rebels did not isolate Suetonius from the rest of his province by preventing him from going south to Londinium, and Suetonius did not attack the rebels and collect his IXth legion.

Once passed the Fosse Way, Suetonius's next concern would have been whether there was a rebel army barring his way at Verulamium. Presumably there was not, because he appears to have reached that city without coming up against any significant resistance. Which is quite surprising really. The Catuvellauni were the only tribe in the eastern counties to have put up any serious resistance to the invading Romans in AD43, and one would have expected them to have been still seething with discontent, and only too ready to rise up, lay Verulamium to waste and kick the foreigners out. But that does not appear to have happened. Perhaps the Catuvellauni had had all their aggression knocked out of them. Possibly the administration of Verulamium was the antithesis of the one in Camulodunum, and the natives in the area had been so well treated that they did not want to jeopardise their futures by rocking the boat. Whether the inhabitants had already evacuated Verulamium, which, from the archaeological evidence, does not appear to have been strongly fortified, we do not know. Certainly, having arrived there, Suetonius must have promptly abandoned it, because we know he went on to Londinium, which had not then, obviously, been sacked by the stormers of Camulodunum.

Which is even more surprising, because it tells us that Suetonius must have arrived there before, or only a relatively short time after the fall of Camulodunum. There would have been a good road from Colchester to London, and in distance it is not very far, so one would have thought that the 'native horde', having had their appetites well and truly whetted by the sacking of the capital, would have moved pretty quickly to do the same thing to trade-rich, undefended Londinium, before any of the other rebel bands around at the time beat them to it.

Anyway, Suetonius had reached his first objective safely. How long would it have taken him to march from Anglesey to Londinium? Once on good Roman roads, his trained troops could have maintained 25, possibly even 30 miles a day without too much difficulty, but perhaps only 10–15 miles a day over mountain tracks. With approximately 200–220 miles to cover, his march to Londinium might therefore have taken between 7 and 11 days. Is that reasonable, or possible?

A thousand years or so later, in 1066, Harold Godwinson, the king of the English, defeated Harold Hardrada, the king of the Danes, at Stamford Bridge, but was down on the south coast to confront William, Duke of Normandy, a little over a week later, having travelled much the same sort of distance – 190 to 200 miles. So it is possible, provided one discounts the view held by some historians that the Anglo-Saxon force was entirely mounted.

Of course, Suetonius might not have used Watling Street. He could have gone south from Wroxeter to Gloucester and Cirencester, and thence to Londinium. It is a longer route, about 280 miles, and it would have taken him another two or three vital days – but it is unlikely that he did go that way, for if he had he would have been able to collect all the garrisons of the Welsh forts en route. However, it would appear, from what Tacitus will shortly tell us, that those garrisons travelled independently, and joined him later.

Having reached Londinium safely, was Suetonius still a worried man? Yes. Dio Cassius tells us:

> However, he was not willing to risk conflict with the barbarians immediately, as he feared their numbers and their desperation, but was inclined to postpone battle to a more convenient season. But as he grew short of food and the barbarians pressed relentlessly upon him, he was compelled, contrary to his judgement, to engage them.

He feared their numbers, then. That is understandable. The 'short of food' comment might merely have been the result of his troops having marched light, and too fast for them to have had time to forage for supplies on the way.

What is very significant, though, is that the 'barbarians pressed relentlessly upon him'. Perhaps his rear guard was being harassed and attacked by the vanguard of Boudicca's army, which might by then have been following him down Watling Street, or possibly the barbarians were bands of rebels from the Welsh or other tribes, cheered and greatly encouraged by the sight of a Roman army in hurried retreat.

Tacitus now has something to tell us in the *Annals* about Londinium:

> This town did not rank as a Roman settlement, but was an important centre for business-men and merchandise. At first, he hesitated whether to stand and fight there.

Those last few words ought finally to settle that earlier question. Suetonius would not have been able to hesitate about whether to stand and fight anywhere, if his army had not been with him. Tacitus continues:

> Eventually, his numerical inferiority – and the price only too clearly paid by the divisional commander's rashness [we have assumed that refers to poor old Cerialis and his thrashed IXth legion] decided him to sacrifice the single city of Londinium to save the province as a whole. [Oh dear, London's a city now, is it? It wasn't a minute ago. Never mind.] Unmoved by lamentations and appeals, Suetonius gave the signal for departure. The inhabitants were allowed to accompany him. But those who stayed because they were women, or old, or attached to the place, were slaughtered by the enemy. Verulamium suffered the same fate.

So Suetonius gave the signal for departure, but which way did he go?

Those historians who are convinced that the final battle took place in the Midlands, naturally want him to head back up north, and they use Tacitus's words 'Verulamium suffered the same fate' to support their argument by claiming that the rebels, having sacked Londinium, must then have followed Suetonius north, and sacked Verulamium on the way. However, there is nothing in Tacitus's words to suggest that that event happened either before or after the sacking of Londinium, and those same historians conveniently ignore the barbarians who, Dio told us, had been pressing Suetonius relentlessly on his march to Londinium. It doesn't matter whether those barbarians were Boudicca's troops or not, they would surely have been the ones who sacked Verulamium. They wouldn't have missed out on that chance of easy booty. If Suetonius had headed north he would have had to fight those barbarian rebels, and force his way through them, but we are told that he did not want to fight a battle, so therefore he would not have gone back the way he had come.

The fact that the inhabitants of Londinium were allowed to accompany him also confirms the statement that he did not want to fight, and had no real expectation of fighting anyone anyway. Hard-headed generals do not usually take a horde of useless civilians along with them to slow them down, eat their supplies, and hamper the movements of their troops. So presumably Suetonius was not expecting to go very far with them.

He would not then have gone north, and neither would he have gone eastwards, towards Camulodunum, where, according to Tacitus, in his *Annals*:

> *The natives enjoyed plundering and thought of nothing else. Bypassing forts and garrisons, they made for where loot was richest and protection weakest. Roman and provincial deaths at the places mentioned are estimated at seventy thousand. For the British did not take or sell prisoners, or practise other war-time exchanges. They could not wait to cut throats, hang, burn, and crucify – as though avenging, in advance, the retribution that was on its way.*

If Suetonius had crossed the Thames he could then have gone west towards Devon and Cornwall, but that would have brought him no apparent advantages. East to Dover would be his last resort, so that only leaves the south, and the big question – what was the client King Cogidumnus going to do?

Suetonius's scouts would probably already have returned to him with the answer. We know the essence of it because Tacitus told us earlier, in the *Agricola,* that Cogidumnus 'maintained his unswerving loyalty down to our own times'. Of course Suetonius must have gone south. It was the only sensible thing for him to do. That business of whether he went north, east or west may seem to have been a waste of time, but at least it was a proper consideration of his options.

It would not be surprising, though, if Cogidumnus were to have told Suetonius that, although he himself would remain loyal to Rome, if the rebels were allowed to encroach too far into his territory, then some of his tribes might be terrorised into joining them, rather than face being slaughtered or having their lands laid to waste. That would have put pressure on Suetonius to stand and fight.

We might also wonder if Cogidumnus, being surely Suetonius's flavour of the month at that moment, used the opportunity to gain political concessions for himself, such as an exemption from repaying Claudius's so-called loan, and possibly confirmation that his heirs would not be treated in the same way that Prasutagus's had been.

That is probably fair comment, but there is a far more important question about Cogidumnus's role in affairs at this point in time which needs consideration.

In war there are allies, enemies and neutrals. Cogidumnus was obviously not an enemy, but neither does neutrality warrant Tacitus's words 'unswerving loyalty'. So he must then have been a fully committed Roman ally.

Ought we therefore to assume that, on hearing of the Iceni revolt, Cogidumnus set about raising an armed force of his own, with which to support the Romans, or defend himself and his kingdom? It would make good sense if he had, and be very surprising if he hadn't. If the other British client kingdom – that of the Iceni – had been organised in such a way that it could readily raise an effective fighting force, as its defeat of the IXth legion clearly demonstrates, then presumably Cogidumnus and his tribes could have done likewise.

If there was a loyalist Regni army in being, why do we not read of it being prepared to fight alongside Suetonius's legionaries? We have come across the Roman ability to manipulate the reporting of events to suit their own purposes before, so it is possible that Cogidumnus did have an army, which did fight on the Roman side, and did help win the day, but whose significant involvement was hushed up, in order to make the victory a singularly Roman one.

Anyway, Suetonius's negative or cautious mood suddenly seems to have disappeared. Tacitus explains why in the *Annals*:

> Suetonius collected the fourteenth brigade and detachments of the twentieth, together with the nearest available auxiliaries – amounting to nearly ten thousand armed men . . .

So Suetonius suddenly had another 10,000 troops to add to his Anglesey field army, which we've already estimated may have numbered about 6,000 men. Where did all those other troops come from?

We have assumed that Suetonius sent out messages and instructions to all his outlying forts before leaving Anglesey. This is partially confirmed when Tacitus later tells us that a message was sent to the IInd legion's headquarters in the Exeter area, instructing those troops to join Suetonius somewhere. It seems reasonable to assume that the same messenger, or others with a similar purpose, would have given identical instructions to all the forts in the Midlands and Welsh border regions, through which they would have had to pass as he or they went down the Wroxeter–Gloucester road, towards Exeter. Those garrisons probably marched via Cirencester and Silchester, to a rendezvous which may have been a little south of Londinium, in Cogidumnus's territory. That is also the best explanation of the word 'collected'. Suetonius did not physically go and get them, he had sent messages for them to come to a rendezvous, and he collected them from there. That is probably where the XIVth brigade and at least one of the detachments of the XXth came from. What about the numbers?

We had assumed that Suetonius's Anglesey army would have consisted of detachments from the XIVth and XXth, and guessed that it numbered about 6,000. That would have left those two legions with garrison strengths still of about 3,000 troops each. If they had all marched in accordance with Suetonius's presumed message, then they also would have numbered 6,000 – less those troops based at the XIVth's HQ, at Wroxeter, who would obviously have joined Suetonius when he went south down Watling Street. So, perhaps 5,000 came to the rendezvous. Auxiliaries are rarely numbered, and how many were the nearest available is anyone's guess, but let us say, for the purpose of this exercise, that there was one auxiliary for every three legionaries, and round that to 2,000. That makes 7,000. So where did the rest come from?

Not from the IInd legion. Tacitus will tell us that they never left the West Country. They were not from the IXth legion either – they were presumably still bottled up in Lincolnshire. How about those ex-XXth legion veterans from Camulodunum – the ones Dio might be accusing of 'betraying' the city? If they had avoided being massacred in Camulodunum, and had turned up to join Suetonius, he must have been delighted. How many veterans were there? We had already guessed that there may have been between 2,500 and 3,500, which fits very nicely – and very conveniently. Now we can mess that calculation right up. Tacitus's words make rather ambiguous English. In this particular paragraph there is a dash at each end of a vital phrase, and therefore '. . . the nearest available auxiliaries – amounting to nearly ten thousand armed men –' might just mean that there were 10,000 nearest available armed auxiliaries.

Native British troops would be referred to by the Romans as auxiliaries, and that many could surely only have come from King Cogidumnus.

Maybe they were the Regni army we had supposed the king might have raised. In which case my apologies to Tacitus for saying they were not mentioned.

Suetonius's army might therefore have suddenly grown to a total of about 26,000 troops although it might be wiser to be cautious about the significance of dashes and simply say that his army's strength may have risen to at least 16,000, or perhaps as many as 26,000 men.

One can understand now why Suetonius's mood must have brightened considerably. Things had not turned out as bad as his worst-case scenario. He'd got to Londinium without mishap. With certain reservations he could retreat into the safe area of Cogidumnus's territory, and he could certainly draw supplies from it. In addition to all that, he had been strongly reinforced, and he may also have been heartened by reports from those of his scouts probing into the Camulodunum and Londinium areas, telling him that the bulk of the rebel army there were acting with no more military precision than a rabble.

Gone now was the hesitancy of whether to stand and fight – or not. Tacitus relates in the *Annals*:

> *Suetonius collected the fourteenth brigade and detachments of the twentieth, together with the nearest available auxiliaries – amounting to nearly ten thousand armed men – and decided to attack without further delay.*

The last part of which is not true at all. He was sensibly seeking the advantage of a good defensive position, where he could wait for his enemies to come to him, on ground of his own choosing. If he was doing that, then Queen Boudicca and her rebel army, reinforced presumably by those native hordes who had sacked Camulodunum and perhaps Londinium, could not have been very far behind him. Tacitus continues:

> *He chose a position in a defile with a wood behind him. There could be no enemy, he knew, except at his front, where there was open country without cover for ambushes.*

So now we come to the million dollar question, or should that be the forty million sesterces question? Where was this defile? Where was the battle going to be fought? Our sources do not give us a location, so we must see what reason and logic can do.

We have surmised that Suetonius would not have wanted the rebels to put pressure on King Cogidumnus by advancing too far into his territory, particularly towards the Chichester area where we suppose the Regni capital was. To do that he would have needed to block Stane Street, the Roman road from Londinium to Chichester, which roughly follows the line of the present A24. So that might be one of the battle site's co-ordinates – somewhere along the A24. We also have that other snippet of information, about the IInd legion not leaving Exeter. We know that the IInd would not come, but Suetonius would not necessarily have known it at the time. If that legion had gathered its outpost detachments and come to the rendezvous, as it seems he instructed them to do, they might well have brought him at least a further 6,000 heavily armoured Roman legionaries. Suetonius would have wanted them, and he would surely have delayed fighting the battle for as long as he could, to give them a chance to arrive. The route he might have expected them to follow may have been from Exeter towards Dorchester, then via Old Sarum to Silchester, and thus east on the North Downs Track Way. So, still hoping they might yet arrive, Suetonius may have chosen a site not far from where that Track Way crosses the A24. That would have had the additional advantage of enabling him to retreat to Dover and Gaul if the battle were to go seriously wrong, because Dover or Richborough is where that track way ultimately leads.

So, perhaps the battle site was near the A24, past Leatherhead, in Box Hill country – not far from the North Downs Track Way, where there are several defiles queueing up for attention.

That is reasoned guesswork, but reason and logic cannot be relied on to fill all the gaps left in history. Wherever the battle was sited, the story should be relatively straightforward from now on, shouldn't it? Well, no – it isn't.

CHAPTER XII

The Battle

Dio gives us an account of the battle, and so too does Tacitus, but apart from an obvious agreement on who the two protagonists were, and the outcome, there is little similarity about them. In fact you might well wonder whether they are describing the same event.

Tacitus's account is the one we are probably most familiar with, so we'll take his first from the *Annals*:

> He . . . decided to attack without further delay. Suetonius drew up his regular troops in close order, with the light-armed auxiliaries at their flanks, and the cavalry massed on the wings.
>
> On the British side, cavalry and infantry bands seethed over a wide area in unprecedented numbers. Their confidence was such that they brought their wives with them to see the victory, installing them in carts stationed at the edge of the battlefield.

Tacitus, and pretty well all of his subsequent readers, seem to have assumed that this business of lining the edge of the battlefield on the rebel side with wives in carts was due to foolish over-confidence on the part of Queen Boudicca and her army, which rebounded on them later when they tried to flee. That is not necessarily a correct explanation of why those carts might have been placed where they were.

There is an incident in Caesar's *Conquest of Gaul*, when in 58BC the Romans were fighting some German tribes led by a man named Ariovistus, which reads:

> The enemy was now compelled to lead his forces out [they consisted of seven different tribes] . . . So that there might be no hope of escaping by flight, they formed a barrier of carriages and wagons along the rear of their whole line, and in them placed their women, who as the men marched to battle stretched out their hands and implored them with tears not to let them be enslaved by the Romans.

So perhaps Queen Boudicca and her military advisers had serious doubts about the fighting resolve of some of the various tribes and troops making up their rebel army, and so placed those wagons and carts with the same purpose as Ariovistus – that of trying to prevent any irresolute warriors from running away as soon as the battle commenced or became difficult.

The next part of Tacitus's account is about Queen Boudicca driving round in her chariot exhorting and encouraging her troops, and that is followed by Suetonius's own oratory to his troops. Both of these speeches were probably concocted by Tacitus, and they can be read in full in the Appendix. However, the last few lines from Suetonius's speech describe very well the Roman method of fighting, which is of interest, and it also refers, perhaps, to a group of people to whom we have already given a great deal of attention:

> 'Just keep in close order. Throw your javelins, and then carry on, use shield-bosses to fell them, swords to kill them. Do not think of plunder. When you have won, you will have everything.'
>
> The General's words were enthusiastically received; the old battle-experienced soldiers longed to hurl their javelins. [Are these old battle-experienced soldiers those veterans of the XXth from Camulodunum?] So Suetonius confidently gave the signal for battle.

Which again cannot be true, because, as we've said before, he was holding the defensive position – and therefore he had to wait for the rebels to attack him, which they duly did.

> At first the regular troops stood their ground. Keeping to the defile as a natural defence, they launched their javelins accurately at the approaching enemy. Then, in wedge formation, they burst forward. So did the auxiliary infantry. The cavalry, too, with lances extended, demolished all serious resistance. The remaining Britons fled with difficulty since their ring of wagons blocked the outlets. The Romans did not spare even the women. Baggage animals too, transfixed with weapons, added to the heaps of dead.
>
> It was a glorious victory, comparable with bygone triumphs. According to one report almost eighty thousand Britons fell. Our own casualties were about four hundred dead and a slightly larger number of wounded.

A cool, brief account, almost a standard account of the triumph of disciplined, well-armoured Roman troops over ill-disciplined and ill-armed natives. So standard an account, in fact, that we can add some details ourselves, if we wish to. The Romans would have waited patiently in lines two or three deep for the rebels to come to close quarters, then the infantry would, at the appropriate moment, have launched each of their two javelins into the rebels' front ranks. The sharp barbed points of those javelins would have pierced either shields or flesh, but then the weight of the wooden shafts would have caused the soft iron of the stems behind the barbs to bend, making it difficult for the javelins to be withdrawn, and impossible for them to be thrown back effectively. Shields thus penetrated would have become too cumbersome to hold up, and most would have to be discarded. The rebel front ranks, those still alive, many having lost their shields, would have become a confused mass that was forced forward by the weight of the numbers behind. They would then have come up against a solid wall of well-armoured Romans, whose short swords would stab through the narrow gaps between their shields into the unprotected flesh of the rebels. When they were ready, those Roman ranks would move relentlessly forward, thrusting out the heavy shields on their left arms like stunning hammer blows, stabbing all the while between them with their swords, and stamping down with their hob-nailed boots or sandals on their fallen foes, making sure they would never rise again alive, until the rebels broke and ran. At which time the lighter-armed auxiliaries and cavalry would have come into their own and completed the rout. A typical Roman victory. The only thing to differentiate this from any of dozens of other reported Roman battles is the description of the site – the defile with a wood behind – open country to the front, and the ring of wagons.

Let us now consider the battle according to Dio Cassius.

> *Boudicca, at the head of an army of about 230,000 men, rode in a chariot herself and assigned the others to their several stations.*

These numbers are too large to be credible. However, when the rebellion started, Dio gave Boudicca an Iceni army of 120,000. That has now almost doubled. If the error factor is consistent, and those numbers can tell us anything at all, and they probably can't, it would be that proportionally the Iceni alone formed more than half of the rebel army. The Trinovantes, Coritani, Catuvellauni, Ordovices, Silures, and any from Anglesey and the Brigantes, thus provided relatively few in proportion to the Iceni contingent, which is surprising. Either there was not enough time for them all to mobilise effectively, or their commitment to the rebellion was far less enthusiastic or widespread than our Roman sources have suggested. Dio continues:

> *Paulinus could not extend his line the whole length of hers, for, even if the men had been drawn up only one deep, they would not have reached far enough, so inferior were they in numbers; nor, on the other hand, did he dare join battle in a single compact force, for fear of being surrounded and cut to pieces. He therefore separated his army into three divisions, in order to fight at several points at one and the same time, and he made each of the divisions so strong that it could not easily be broken through.*

109

It is difficult to understand just what Dio is telling us here. One wonders if he really knew himself. Forming three separate divisions would not have prevented each of them being surrounded and attacked on all sides. And how could they have been made so strong that they could not easily be broken through, unless perhaps barricades were thrown up? But that cannot be right, since they would then have been unable to manoeuvre. Perhaps the outer ranks of each division were made up entirely of the more heavily armoured legionaries, and the end result was something more akin to the nineteenth-century squares used when infantry faced a cavalry attack, or even the old Greek-style armoured phalanxes, with javelins instead of long spears. It is an interesting proposition for the military historian, and the imagination.

What follows is a lengthy speech in which, no doubt, Dio says what he thinks Suetonius would have said to his troops – but three times, because he has created a different speech for each division. We will consign all those to the Appendix.

Note that there is no mention of a defensive position in a defile. Dio may, in fact, be telling us that, as far as he knew, there were no physical features guarding the Roman army's flanks. Dio continues:

After addressing these and like words to them he raised the signal for battle. Thereupon the armies approached each other, the barbarians with much shouting mingled with menacing battle-songs, but the Romans silently and in order until they came within a javelin's throw of the enemy. Then, while their foes were still advancing against them at a walk, the Romans rushed forward at a signal and charged them at full speed, and when the clash came, easily broke through the opposing ranks; but, as they were surrounded by the great numbers of the enemy, they had to be fighting everywhere at once. Their struggle took many forms. Light-armed troops exchanged missiles with light-armed, heavy-armed were opposed to heavy-armed, cavalry clashed with cavalry, and against the chariots of the barbarians the Roman archers contended. The barbarians would assail the Romans with a rush of their chariots, knocking them helter-skelter, but, since they fought without breastplates, would themselves be repulsed by the arrows. Horseman would overthrow foot-soldier and foot-soldier strike down horseman; a group of Romans, forming in close order, would advance to meet the chariots, and others would be scattered by them; a band of Britons would come to close quarters with the archers and rout them, while others were content to dodge their shafts at a distance; and all this was going on not at one spot only, but in all three divisions at once.

They contended for a long time, both parties being animated by the same zeal and daring. But finally, late in the day, the Romans prevailed; and they slew many in battle beside the wagons and the forest, and captured many alive.

Nevertheless, not a few made their escape and were preparing to fight again.

In the meantime, however, Boudicca fell sick and died. The Britons mourned her deeply and gave her a costly burial; but, feeling that now at last they were really defeated, they scattered to their homes. So much for the affairs in Britain.

There we have the two accounts of Queen Boudicca's battle of Britain. Tacitus makes out that the victory was a relatively easy one. Dio states that it was a hard and long fight, and mentions the part played by chariots and Roman archers in the battle. We must now try to work out, if that is indeed possible, which is the more reliable.

Tacitus is given plus points because it is assumed that he had his account from Agricola, whose memory of what was probably his first major battle ought to have been fixed more vividly in his mind than any of those he may have been in later. However, we do not have a vivid account – we have one which is clinically brief, and with no personally witnessed anecdotes. So, for the young and inexperienced Agricola, the battle may just have been confused mayhem. Perhaps the only clear features still in his mind some twenty or thirty years later, when he was talking to his son-in-law, were the wooded defile, the plain, and the wagons.

What about Dio then? His account of the battle is rarely if ever alluded to, so modern historians have few plus points to give him. Yet, if Dio had delved into the Roman imperial archives for AD60 and discovered Decianus's report mentioning the repayment of Claudius's and Seneca's loans, which he surely must have done, what other documents on British affairs did he come across? Perhaps when Dio was writing his version of the battle he may not only have had Tacitus's books before him, but also Suetonius's official reports and other eye-witness accounts as well. Should we then consider very seriously the possibility that Dio found Tacitus's account differed so much from his other sources that he decided it was inaccurate, and wrote down what he perceived to be the correct version?

Or did he just create a more interesting version for his audiences or readers? Some parts of Dio's account of the battle for Britain in AD60 do bear an uncanny resemblance to the close-quarter fighting of Homer's Greeks and Trojans, and there are also similarities, at least with the three divisional split, to a battle fought by Agricola against the Caledonians, many years later. Did Dio get the battle mixed up with another one, as we suspect he may have done earlier with Vespasian and his son? Or, alternatively, was it Tacitus who had it all wrong?

If this all boils down simply to a question of the accuracy of our two sources, then Dio ought to come out on top. That Vespasian incident is the only fault we have found in his narrative so far, and it is only a minor one, whereas with Tacitus we have two clear-cut examples of contradiction, the first about the garrisoning of Anglesey, and the second over the rebels storming or not storming forts. In addition, his handling of the Camulodunum story, and with it the timing of the IXth legion's battle, is both clumsy and confused, and he duplicated the Venutius/Cartimandua story and got one version completely out of its chronological sequence. Also, on the important matter of research, he could not have delved into archives that perhaps were still closed to him, to the same extent that Dio did or else he would have known about Seneca's loan and Decianus's debacle with the so-called Claudian gifts.

The truth is that this is a debate which cannot be positively resolved – nevertheless, it is difficult to keep a completely open mind. I am inclined to think that Dio is probably the safer historian, but the Roman forces in his account do not fight in the disciplined, well-drilled way one might have expected them to. So perhaps I tend to favour Tacitus, although I doubt very much if the Roman victory was as easy as he makes out. Let us move on.

We can deal with the aftermath of the battle later, but firstly we should finalise our deliberations on its site, now that we have read both accounts. We had Tacitus's defile, and open plain, and we can now add the need for there to have been a reasonably good road nearby, otherwise those carts and wagons would have presented all sorts of problems travelling across country. Dio briefly mentions 'woods' and 'carts', and, in a way, he confirms Tacitus's open plain, since his battlefield was level enough to be suitable for the extensive use of chariots.

That must eliminate the academically favoured East Midlands site of Mancetter, for there, between where the Roman troops and the rebels must have taken up their battle stations, runs the River Anker, and Watling Street with its raised *agger* platform and its drainage ditches to either side. Those would all have been serious hazards to the rebels and their chariots when they attacked, and 'tank traps' for the Roman infantry when they charged, and it hardly fits the description of an open plain anyway.

Defile or no defile, a site south of London, near the ancient chalk ridge track way still seems as good as any, but only the unlikely discovery of a mass burial, associated with closely identifiable armour, coins or weapons, would pinpoint the actual place or area. The Romans, however, would never have deliberately buried armour or weapons, either theirs or the rebels', in such a situation – they were too valuable a commodity, and if any of the bones have survived a 2,000-year interment in chalky ground, dating them so precisely would be a near impossibility. In other words, any such site, if it were found, would still be controversial and open to dispute.

Dio has said his piece on the rebellion now, so what does the terse Tacitus have to say next in the *Annals*?

Boudicca poisoned herself.

So our sources are again in conflict. Dio had said that 'Boudicca fell sick and died. The Britons mourned her deeply and gave her a costly burial.'

Recently an eminent historian, fronting a series of television programmes on British history, stated positively that Boudicca committed suicide to prevent herself falling into Roman hands. A similarly worded answer to a question on University Challenge was also accepted as being correct. Has no one else read Dio Cassius? Or is there a conspiracy by academics to promote only Tacitus's version of those events on which he and Dio disagree? If so, that is hardly the correct way to present a balanced view of historical events. It is not a question of earth-shattering importance, but which of our two sources might be right on this occasion?

It may have been the fashion for Romans in Rome to commit suicide with poison if they were already doomed by imperial decree – that being a preferable option to other more unpleasant ways of dying. But Queen Boudicca was not a Roman, and there is nothing to suggest that suicide was ever part of Celtic tradition. On the contrary, death in battle was preferable, even for a woman perhaps, since it may have brought an entree into a better next life. Anyway, why should Boudicca have committed suicide when she surely still had her freedom? She would have been well mounted or charioted, and probably surrounded by a strong bodyguard made up of the best Iceni warriors, so she and they ought to have had no trouble in getting well clear of the governor's clutches. And they would not have been alone. Dio said: '. . . not a few made their escape and were preparing to fight again.' Which is precisely what one would expect, and 'not a few' rebels could well mean quite a lot of rebels.

It is difficult to imagine that someone like Boudicca, with the guts to take on the might of Rome, would have given up so easily while most of East Anglia was still effectively in rebel hands, and while the possibility of raising another army still existed. It is also very unlikely that Suetonius would have permitted his precious army to split up into small groups and pursue the fleeing British initially, for fear that his troops might be ambushed or set upon as darkness fell, by desperate rebels who had reformed, or were acting as a formal rear guard. So why did Tacitus say what he did?

Well, he used a couple of one-line sentences quite erroneously a little while back, presumably for dramatic effect – those which stated that Suetonius was going to attack, when Suetonius so obviously was not going to attack. Perhaps 'Boudicca poisoned herself' is yet another of those dramatic sentences, written to tidy things up in a manner he thought more acceptable to the minds of his Roman audiences.

So in this instance I definitely favour the words of Dio. The mention of the deep mourning, the costly burial, and her death finally bringing despair to her followers, give his words a ring of veracity that Tacitus's lack.

Poor Boudicca, until recently a pampered queen, used to being waited on hand and foot, had spent many weeks, probably roughing it in the open in all weathers, acting the part of a tough leader of a rebellion, eating a poor diet, and maybe risking dysentery or worse by drinking bad water. After the trauma of witnessing the defeat of her troops, it would not be surprising if she fell sick after a panic stricken flight, and subsequently died. She must have been a very brave woman to have accomplished what she had, and it is nice to know that her followers gave her a good funeral.

Having dutifully said all that, this is surely one occasion when those who are romantics at heart can overrule both of our conflicting historical sources in favour of the totally unfounded proposition that she did not die just then, and that the story of her demise was given out so that the Romans would not pursue her. She might, with her two daughters, have fled back to Norfolk, picked up whatever jewels, clothes and other wealth she could lay her hands on, and then have taken ship, and gone back home – to her mum and dad – if they were still alive, in Caledonia, or Scotland as it is now.

If she did, she missed picking up all those gold torcs at Snettisham, but what is this about Queen Boudicca being a Scot? Surely that is taking romance too far beyond the bounds of credulity? Well, Queen Boudicca was, we are told, of royal blood, but she was obviously not of Iceni royal blood, since Prasutagus, her husband, was king, not consort, and when he died it was to his daughters that he left half of his kingdom. So, which part of Britain did Boudicca come from?

Dio might have given us a clue in his earlier description of her. He must almost certainly have dug it out of the archives or lifted it from an eye-witness account, because it contains far too much detail for it to have been only a figment of his imagination – and the observations about her clothing must surely have been made by a woman who had met or seen her.

> *In stature she was very tall, in appearance most terrifying, in the glance of her eye most fierce, and her voice was harsh; a great mass of the tawniest hair fell to her hips; around her neck was a large golden necklace; and she wore a tunic of divers colours over which a thick mantle was fastened with a brooch. This was her invariable attire.*

Now read again what Tacitus wrote earlier in the *Agricola*, when he was describing the inhabitants of Britain, and speculating on where they may have come from.

The reddish hair and large limbs of the Caledonians proclaim a German origin.

Boudicca definitely had the red tawny hair, and the large limbs – so, according to Tacitus, she could have been a Caledonian Scot. On the other hand, you might point out that Tacitus actually said that 'red hair and large limbs . . . proclaim a German origin', and that Prasutagus was more likely to have had an association with such people in northern Europe, through trade across the North Sea, than with tribes in Scotland. Perhaps that is so, but Dio had also earlier told us that she was a 'Briton woman', so that rules out her being a German or northern European.

Is it not also significant that the large golden necklace is probably a description of a Celtic torc? Or that the tunic of divers colours might have been made of a tartan material? The origins of woven multi-coloured tartan style cloth go much farther back in Celtic history than this period – it is only in the seventeenth and eighteenth centuries that clans started adopting specific patterns. That thick mantle too – fastened with a brooch – could that not be a plaid? All this, Dio tells us, with just a hint of feminine acidity, was her 'invariable attire', so it was not just donned for the occasion.

Convinced? It is good circumstantial evidence, but perhaps we should just say that Britain's most famous heroine may have been a Scot, and leave it at that. What else can we tentatively say about her?

Most probably Boudicca's marriage was, like many later royal weddings, arranged for diplomatic reasons. She and her future husband may never have met before, and when she turned up to become Prasutagus's bride, she was probably young – perhaps only 14 or 15 years old. To the rest of the Iceni tribe she would have been a stranger from a foreign land, who probably did not even speak their language. Even now, in Norfolk, newcomers are sometimes regarded with suspicion, and if they are not exactly ostracised, they are not often overtly welcomed, and so it may well have been then. For Boudicca to have subsequently endeared herself to Prasutagus's subjects to such an extent that they were prepared to allow her to lead them into war, and then fight and die in her name, indicates that she must have had an exceptionally charismatic personality.

We can be certain that she and Prasutagus had no living son, or else the realm would have been left to him. We do not know if the two daughters were the only children Boudicca had, but if they were, and they were still too young to have been diplomatically married off in turn, we might also assume that the elder was not yet 14. In which case Queen Boudicca might only have been about 30 years old when she died, if that was indeed in AD60. Anyway, she has gone from the scene now, unfortunately, and her army has disbanded, or at least scattered, and Tacitus needs to officially tidy up a loose end, the essence of which we have already taken out of order several times. In the *Annals*:

> *Poenius Postumus, chief-of-staff of the IInd legion which had not joined Suetonius, learning of the success of the other two formations, stabbed himself to death because he had cheated his formation of its share in the victory and had broken regulations by disobeying his commander's orders.*

It is from this passage, with its 'other two formations', which Tacitus has already told us contained significant numbers of the XIVth and XXth legionaries, that we know for certain that none of the IXth or the IInd could have been present at the main battle. We are not specifically told that the IInd legion did not join Suetonius because they were being blockaded by rebels, but it is difficult to believe that the governor's orders would have been disobeyed by an experienced senior officer for no good reason. But if we are wrong, it doesn't matter very much – it would only reduce the number of tribes who might possibly have joined the rebellion, and illustrate the incalculable effect pure chance might have on a military campaign.

Either way, it was bad luck on poor Poenius. If the chief-of-staff was in charge, then the IInd legion's real commander must have been away on official business, perhaps with Suetonius. Poenius may have been over cautious, but he would have been wiser to have risked defeat or heavy loses by having some sort of battle with the rebel Dumnonii or Durotriges, if they really had mobilised in some force near Exeter for the purpose of preventing his legion from joining Suetonius. If the governor had also sent marching orders to Cerialis, as is most likely, then those orders too were disobeyed. However, Cerialis had friends in high places, and that is perhaps why he was able to get away with not only disobeying orders, but also his earlier rash action with its high casualties. Poenius, on the other hand, may only have been a sound and steady career soldier who had risen from the ranks. With no old school tie to help him, he would probably have been on a hiding to nothing whatever he did. Still, one would have thought that stabbing himself to death was going a bit over the top. It would probably have been a lot less painful for him if he'd taken some of Tacitus's poison.

CHAPTER XIII
The Aftermath

The loss of the battle, and the death of Queen Boudicca did not end the rebellion. That should not surprise us. There must have been many individuals in Boudicca's Iceni entourage, or chiefs of other tribes, who were perfectly capable of leading military units or bands of some size, who through sheer desperation had little choice but to continue to fight on in the hope that a new rebel army and a new charismatic leader might suddenly appear from somewhere. Certainly capitulation or capture would probably have resulted in instant slaughter by the outraged Romans.

Initially, of course, the whole of present-day East Anglia, the Home Counties and most of the Midlands were still in rebel hands, but it would only have been a matter of time before those solid, fearsome Roman legions turned up again. No doubt the more cautious of those rebel bands would have set out to seek some sort of safety well away from eastern England in the wilder regions of the Welsh mountains or the Brigantes' territories in the Pennines. Those rebels who remained would have needed to be very alert and mobile to avoid disaster, and to fight like the devil if cornered.

Tacitus's account of what happened after the main battle rushes on far too quickly for comfort, leaving many questions unanswered, and certainly we get no British viewpoint. In his *Annals* he says:

> *The whole army was now united. Suetonius kept it under canvas to finish the war.*

It would have been nice to know if Suetonius had to march all the way down to Exeter to get the late Poenius's IInd legion off their backsides, and then march all the way up the Fosse Way into Lincolnshire to prise the remnants of Cerialis's IXth legion out from behind their fortifications. There must have been some red faces in both camps when Suetonius eventually turned up and let rip with some choice Latin swear words.

There are several possible reasons why the army might have been kept under canvas. If we were right, and the garrisons of both the XXth and the

117

XIVth did abandon their forts and outposts in the Welsh borders, we might also assume that the delighted Silures and Ordovices promptly burned them to the ground. Some of the fortifications of the IXth legion too may have been destroyed or seriously damaged, and we can be pretty certain that Camulodunum's XXth veterans would have had no homes to return to. Londinium and Verulamium were also flattened, so, with the exception presumably of the IInd's forts and garrisons, all of the rest of Suetonius's army may have had no choice but to sleep under canvas.

Clearly though, Suetonius obviously still feared the possibility of another rebel army gathering somewhere to threaten him. There is also a hint here that Suetonius might have felt that some of his army and its generals had let him down badly during the early part of that summer by acting slowly, rashly, or not at all, and he may have wanted to keep them all closely under his thumb. However, Tacitus's statement that the Roman army was kept united ought to be questioned. If Suetonius had abandoned many of his forts, the borders of his province would have been largely undefended, and one would have expected the tribes in those areas to have taken full advantage of that, and to have gone on the rampage, creating even more mayhem, just when Suetonius needed things to quieten down. So possibly those outposts were rebuilt and re-garrisoned fairly quickly.

However, there was some good news for Suetonius from the continent. He wasn't being given the sack, and neither did he need to reach for his flask of poison. Nero had apparently accepted his explanations about the origins of the revolt, perhaps because it was his own money-grabbing policies that had caused the problem in the first place. Anyway, the emperor was signalling his confidence in his commander-in-chief, and his army. From the *Annals*:

> The emperor raised its numbers by transferring from Germany two thousand regular troops, which brought the ninth division to full strength, also eight auxiliary infantry battalions and a thousand cavalry.

We do not know how many casualties the Roman army suffered in total during those months. The IXth may have lost the most in its earlier battle with the Iceni, and subsequently when or if some of their forts were stormed, but there would have been more deaths in the fighting at Anglesey as well as the reported 400 in the main battle, plus an even larger number of injured who might never be fit enough to fight again. Some of those losses may already have been made good by temporarily re-enlisting at least the younger of those Camulodunum veterans, who after all, now had no homes to go to, and any surplus may then have been drafted to the IXth, before the two thousand from Germany turned up.

Tacitus now tells us a little more about those newly arrived two thousand troops which were attached to the IXth legion. The *Annals* again:

These were stationed together in new winter quarters, and hostile or wavering tribes were ravaged with fire and sword.

So it must have been getting on for winter by the time the troops from Germany arrived, but they at least were not going spend it under canvas. It is possible that Cerialis's camp near Lincoln had been so badly damaged by Iceni assaults that a new one had to be built to house those replacements. That might explain why archaeologists cannot date the one they have excavated earlier than AD60. There may be another older camp site not all that far away – perhaps a mile or two to the north. It is about this time that an important announcement ought to have been made in what passed for the British national media.

With Camulodunum destroyed and Suetonius's main base now being, presumably, still in safe Cogidumnus territory, the ford over the River Thames at Londinium would have become a vital pivot point for pretty well all of Suetonius's operations north of the river. It must have been from about this time that London became *de facto* the strategic centre of Britain. All major roads constructed from then on would lead to or from that place. Once the Al, or Ermine Street, had been constructed to link Londinium directly with Peterborough, Lincoln and the north, then both the Via Devana and Peddars Way would have lost their importance, and would soon have declined to a mere 'B' road status. Their *raison d'être* – Camulodunum's strategic influence and importance – had been destroyed with the colony. That city would be rebuilt, but it would no longer effectively be the administrative capital of Britain.

So, back to the fire and sword business. Do you remember Tacitus's words about the rebels behaviour at Londinium? 'They could not wait to cut throats, hang, burn, and crucify – as though avenging, in advance, the retribution that was on its way.' Well, that forecast retribution was obviously being enacted. There was no Red Cross, Geneva Convention or United Nations mediation then, and when Tacitus says 'fire and sword', he probably meant it.

The Dumnonii and Durotriges of Devon and Cornwall may have prevented poor Poenius's IInd legion from joining Suetonius's army, so fire and sword for them. The Silures, Ordovices and Cornovii may or may not have chased Suetonius to London, or burned those Welsh border forts, but they can go on the list as well. The tribes down Watling Street, mainly the Catuvellauni, were 'disaffected', and even if they do not seem to have whole-heartedly joined in the rebellion – add them too.

All that was probably just like a pre-match warming up session. The Roman vengeance on the Trinovantes would have been terrible, and the

Coritani probably suffered equally badly. However, at the top of the list, undoubtedly, would have been the Iceni. This was the tribe of a client king who had been trusted to support the Roman authorities, and, however justifiable the reasons, had subsequently betrayed that trust. On the Iceni then, is where Suetonius's heavy hand must have fallen with the greatest force. The complete and utter destruction of its towns and villages, and the slaughter or enslavement of almost the entire Iceni native population, might well have been the result. The emperor Trajan did something similar to an errant client kingdom in the country of Dacia, some forty-odd years later. Perhaps it is no wonder that archaeologists have not yet found, to their satisfaction, the real site of Boudicca's palace or capital – it may have been levelled to the ground, and if, as is most likely, it was constructed of wood, then its site may have been completely obliterated.

Ravaging with fire and sword was probably the Roman legionaries' favourite sport, but there would have been some dirty jobs that needed doing. The burned ruins of Londinium, Verulamium and Camulodunum would have to be cleaned up and put back into some sort of order for the re-emerging civil authorities. Such tasks might have been ideal punishments for detachments of the errant IInd legion and maybe the IXth too, leaving the two loyal formations happily plundering the rest of East Anglia. Tacitus probably has his tongue in his cheek when he says in the *Annals*:

> But the enemy's worst affliction was famine. For they had neglected to sow their fields and brought everyone available into the army, intending to seize our supplies.

It is very doubtful whether a desperate people, engaged in the fearful task of setting up a rebellion in which a horrible death would be the reward for failure, would have given too much consideration to where their meals would be coming from six months later. It does rather confirm, though, what we have already suspected, that the rebellion, for the people of the Iceni at least, might have been a total commitment of all classes.

The harried survivors and their families would have had to take refuge in the thick forests or remote meres and fens, where they would eke out a subsistence living if they were lucky. It was a style of existence which was perhaps not too far from the norm for the lower classes of society, and so perhaps they fared better than we or the Romans would have expected. Perhaps hate, fear or desperation drove some of those partisans to act like the Spanish guerrilleros in Napoleon's day, and attack foraging parties and patrols, for Tacitus goes on to say: 'Still, the savage British tribesmen were disinclined for peace.' And so would most of us have been, if surrender meant slavery or an unpleasant, tortured death, but politics had started to come into the equation. Tacitus continues:

> *. . . especially as the newly arrived imperial agent Gaius Julius Alpinus Classicianus, successor to Catus Decianus, was on bad terms with Suetonius, and allowed his personal animosities to damage the national interests. For he passed round advice to wait for a new governor who would be kind to those who surrendered, without an enemy's bitterness or a conqueror's arrogance. Classicianus also reported to Rome that there was no prospect of ending the war unless a successor was appointed to Suetonius, whose failures he attributed to perversity – and his successes to luck.*

Decianus had presumably got the sack, or was conveniently shuffled sideways into some other administrative job in Rome's equivalent of Siberia, but that was only to be expected.

Tacitus was pro-Suetonius, and so his comments about Classicianus are understandable. However, the new imperial agent was clearly not going to be bossed about, and was presumably prepared to tell Suetonius to his face, if they ever got that close, that his fire and sword policy was not the way to settle the province down and get the economy back into shape. One cannot imagine Suetonius liking that advice, and probably, perversely, he would have reacted by grinding the natives down even harder, only to then find that his new agent was going over his head – directly to Nero.

It would seem that there must still have been some sort of structure in the ranks of the rebels, since the new agent, Classicianus, appears to have been in communication with some sort of negotiating, or bargaining team, who were clearly unwilling to deal directly with Suetonius the governor.

There might be another more subtle reason for the continued resistance. Some of the wiser British might have realised that the best chance of ever getting the Romans to pack up and leave, was by trying to make sure that the country's economy never did pick up. If the Rome authorities could be made to think that the unsettled situation would continue indefinitely, they might then decide that Britain was no longer a viable proposition – and withdraw.

How crucial some moments in history are. The rebellion initiated by Queen Boudicca was, quite unexpectedly, within an ace of successfully ousting the Romans from Britain, because Nero was actually thinking along those lines. Suetonius, in *The Twelve Caesars*, says: 'Nero . . . even considered withdrawing his forces from Britain.' Before taking that crucial step, however, it seems that he decided first to send out an independent person to investigate and report on what actually was going on in Britain. Which was very sensible of him. In fact, he doesn't seem to have acted towards his British interests quite like the bloodthirsty, immature idiot his actions in Rome make him out to be. Tacitus again in the *Annals*:

> *So a former slave, Polyclitus, was sent to investigate the British situation.*

> *Nero was very hopeful that Polyclitus's influence would reconcile the governor and agent and pacify native rebelliousness. With his enormous escort, Polyclitus was a trial to Italy and Gaul. Then he crossed the Channel and succeeded in intimidating even the Roman army. But the enemy laughed at him. For them, freedom still lived, and the power of ex-slaves was still unfamiliar. The British marvelled that a general and an army who had completed such a mighty war should obey a slave.*

According to Tacitus, Polyclitus's visit achieved nothing, but he was probably wrong on that score. Someone must have been bending Nero's ear. In the *Annals*:

> *But all this was toned down in Polyclitus' reports to the emperor. Retained as governor, Suetonius lost a few ships and their crews on the shore, and was then superseded for not terminating the war. His successor, the recent consul Publius Petronius Turpilianus, neither provoking the enemy nor provoked, called this ignoble inactivity peace with honour.*

Tacitus also comments in the *Agricola*:

> *But many guilty rebels refused to lay down their arms out of a peculiar dread of the legate [still Suetonius]. Fine officer though he was, he seemed likely to abuse their unconditional surrender and punish with undue severity wrongs which he insisted on making personal. The government therefore replaced him by Petronius Turpilianus. They hoped that he would be more merciful and readier to forgive offences to which he was a stranger . . .*

Nero was probably told by Polyclitus that Suetonius was unable to conceive of anything other than his iron-fist policy, and it was that which was preventing the recovery of the province's economy. So, in AD61 Nero removed him from office. It doesn't seem to have done Suetonius any lasting harm though, because five years later he became a consul in Rome.

Turpilianus must have started his period of governorship in Britain by issuing a general amnesty, or a pardon even, to all those rebels still under arms or in hiding.

In those days of poor mass communication, the amnesty was probably initiated by simply withdrawing the Roman troops from the still affected areas in East Anglia or confining them to their camps. Then one would presume that some trusted tribal representatives would have been sent in to explain that there would be no further retribution, and that the remaining rebels were free to come out of hiding, and start cultivating the land again.

It would seem that now the final ripples from Queen Boudicca's rebellion were effectively stilled.

So why did Queen Boudicca's rebellion fail? At times it seemed almost on the verge of success.

The failure to prevent the garrison troops of both the XIVth and the XXth, together possibly with Camulodunum's XXth veterans, from joining up with Suetonius's Anglesey army was critical. If the Iceni's call to arms had reached Exeter, then it presumably also arrived in Wales, so the Welsh tribes might take some of the blame for that, but, in truth, that merger of the Roman forces south of the Thames could never have taken place anyway, if Boudicca and the Iceni had intercepted and defeated Suetonius's army as it marched down from Anglesey.

Suetonius may have reacted remarkably quickly, but it is unlikely that he would have been able to march so fast that the rebels did not at least have the chance to build barricades and block his way. That they did not must surely have been because they felt their own army had not then grown strong enough to fight the necessary battle, and by the time sufficient numbers had arrived, it was too late. Suetonius had passed the Fosse Way, and was hurrying towards London, and a rendezvous with those significantly strong reinforcements.

It would not be true to simply say that if Suetonius had been defeated at the junction of Watling Street with the Fosse Way, then Queen Boudicca's rebellion would have been assured of victory. The Roman troops that turned up south of Londinium, together perhaps with King Cogidumnus's forces, might still have been able to vanquish a rebel army that would have been much depleted by the casualties suffered in a battle with Suetonius.

The other important factor is that support for the Iceni's rebellion among other tribes, except perhaps in Devon and Essex, seems to have been rather lukewarm. Whether that was due to a reluctance to co-operate, or there was insufficient time for them to gather in significant numbers of forces, we will probably never know. Cogidumnus was obviously too pro-Roman to help anyway, but if the Catuvellauni had been as enthusiastic as the Trinovantes, we might have expected to read about Verulamium and Londinium being sacked or besieged long before we do – and if the Brigantes had taken over the task of blockading the IXth's forts on the Trent, then the Iceni and Coritani forces themselves might just have been powerful enough to face up to Suetonius's Anglesey army on Watling Street.

It all seems to have boiled down to a matter of timing. The rebels took too long to mobilise or to manoeuvre their army into an effective position, and Suetonius's speed of reaction prevented him from being cut off from the rest of his province, and from being forced to fight in disadvantaged circumstances.

Epilogue

We have read of events which took place within a period of only eighteen years or so, yet those years were a crucial period in British history. If Queen Boudicca's rebellion had been successful in driving the Romans out, then who knows what effect that might have had, not only on British history, but on the world as we know it in the twenty-first century? So it is a period that should be much better known and understood.

Queen Boudicca's name is obviously world famous, but much less so is the name Caratacus – and what about Togodumnus, Cogidumnus, Prasutagus, Cartimandua or Venutius? How many people realise that it is just possible that Queen Boudicca was a Scot?

Of the Romans, Agricola's name is best known, but he is often mistakenly thought of as one of the Roman emperors, rather than as a governor of Britain. Few seem to know that the future emperor Vespasian was ever here, or that the general who defeated Boudicca was Suetonius Paulinus, or that the rash Cerialis, who got his troops cut up and massacred by the Iceni, also became a governor of Britain.

Tacitus and Dio Cassius both tell a story that is less well known to the British than the fictitious lives of King Arthur and Robin Hood. It ought not to be so.

Tacitus, with his pen, wove a cloak of immortality which in time came to be spread over himself and Agricola, but in doing so its folds covered many others, and preserved for us a glimpse into a period of our history that we ought to gloat over and treasure.

Appendix

Julius Caesar's account of the geography of Britain

The island is triangular, with one side facing Gaul. One corner of this side, on the coast of Kent, is the landing-place for nearly all the ships from Gaul, and points east; the lower corner points south. The length of this side is about 475 miles. Another side faces west, towards Spain, in this direction is Ireland, which is supposed to be half the size of Britain, and lies at the same distance from it as Gaul. Midway across is the Isle of Man, and it is believed that there are also a number of smaller islands, in which according to some writers there is a month of perpetual darkness at the winter solstice. Our inquiries on this subject were always fruitless, but we found by accurate measurements with a water-clock that the nights are shorter than on the continent. This side of Britain, according to the natives' estimate, is 665 miles long. The third side faces north; no land lies opposite it, but its eastern corner points roughly in the direction of Germany. Its length is estimated at 760 miles. Thus the whole island is 1,900 miles in circumference.

Tacitus's description of the geography of Britain

Though the geographical position and peoples of Britain have been described by many writers, I am going to describe them again, not to match my skill and research against theirs, but because the conquest was only completed in this period. Where my predecessors relied on style to adorn their guesses, I shall offer assured fact. Britain, the largest of the islands known to us Romans, is so shaped and situated as to face Germany on the East and Spain on the West, while to the South it actually lies in full view of Gaul. Its northern shores, with no land confronting them, are beaten by a wild and open sea. The general shape of Britain has been compared by Livy, the best of the old writers, and by Fabius Rusticus, the best of the younger, to an elongated diamond or a double headed axe. Such indeed is its shape south of Caledonia, and so the same shape has been attributed to the whole.

But when you go farther North you find a huge and shapeless tract of country, jutting out towards the land's end and finally tapering into a kind of wedge. This coast of that remotest sea was first rounded, at this time, by a Roman fleet, which thus established the fact that Britain was an island. At the same time it discovered and subdued the Orkney Islands, hitherto unknown. Thule, too, was sighted by our men, but no more; their orders took them no farther, and winter was close at hand. But they do report that the sea is sluggish and heavy to the oar and, even with the wind, does not rise as other seas do. The reason, I suppose, is that lands and mountains, which create and feed storms, are scarcer there and the deep mass of an unbroken sea is more slowly set in motion. To investigate the nature of Ocean and its tides lies outside my immediate scope, and the tale has often been told. I will add just one observation. Nowhere does the sea hold wider sway; it carries to and fro in its motion a mass of currents, and, in its ebb and flow, is not held by the coast, but passes deep inland and winds about, pushing in among highlands and mountains, as if in its own domain.

Dio's rendering of Queen Boudicca's speech to the Iceni tribes urging the rebellion

'You have learned by actual experience how different freedom is from slavery. Hence, although some among you may previously, through ignorance of which was better, have been deceived by the alluring promises of the Romans, yet now that you have tried both, you have learned how great a mistake you made in preferring an imported despotism to your ancestral mode of life, and you have come to realise how much better is poverty with no master than wealth with slavery. For what treatment is there of the most shameful or grievous sort that we have not suffered ever since these men made their appearance in Britain? Have we not been robbed entirely of most of our possessions, and for those the greatest, while for those that remain we pay taxes?

Besides pasturing and tilling for them all our other possessions, do we not pay a yearly tribute for our very bodies? How much better it would be to have been sold to masters once and for all than, possessing empty titles of freedom, to have to ransom ourselves every year! How much better to have been slain and to have perished than to go about with a tax on our heads! Yet why do I mention death? For even dying is not free of cost with them; nay, you know what fees we deposit even for our dead. Among the rest of mankind death frees even those who are in slavery to others; only in the case of the Romans do the very dead remain alive for their profit. Why is it that, though none of us has any money (how, indeed, could we, or where could we get it?), we are stripped and despoiled like a murderer's victims? And why should the Romans be expected to display moderation as time goes on, when they have behaved towards us in this fashion at the very outset, when all men show consideration even for the beasts they have newly captured?

But to speak the plain truth, it is we who have made ourselves responsible for all these evils, in that we allowed them to set foot on the island in the first place instead of expelling them at once as we did their famous Julius Caesar, – yes, and in that we did not deal with them while they were still far away as we dealt with

Augustus and with Gaius Caligula and make even the attempt to sail hither a formidable thing. As a consequence, although we inhabit so large an island, or rather a continent, one might say, that is encircled by the sea, and although we possess a veritable world of our own and are so separated by the ocean from all the rest of mankind that we have been believed to dwell on a different earth and under a different sky, and that some of the outside world, aye, even their wisest men, have not hitherto known for a certainty even by what name we are called, we have, notwithstanding all this, been despised and trampled underfoot by men who know nothing else than how to secure gain.

However, even at this late day, though we have not done so before, let us, my countrymen and friends and kinsmen, – for I consider you all kinsmen, seeing that you inhabit a single island and are called by one common name, – let us, I say, do our duty while we still remember what freedom is, that we may leave to our children not only its appellation but also its reality. For if we utterly forget the happy state in which we were born and bred, what, pray, will they do, reared in bondage?

All this I say, not with the purpose of inspiring you with a hatred of present conditions, – that hatred you already have, – not with fear for the future, – that fear you already have, – but of commending you because you now of your own accord choose the requisite course of action, and of thanking you for so readily co-operating with me and with each other. Have no fear whatever of the Romans; for they are superior to us neither in numbers nor in bravery. And here is the proof, they have protected themselves with helmets and breastplates and greaves and yet further provided themselves with palisades and walls and trenches to make sure of suffering no harm by an incursion of their enemies. For they are influenced by their fears when they adopt this kind of fighting in preference to the plan we follow of rough and ready action. Indeed, we enjoy such a surplus of bravery, that we regard our tents as safer than their walls and our shields as affording greater protection than their whole suits of mail. As a consequence, we when victorious capture them, and when overpowered elude them; and if we ever choose to retreat anywhere, we conceal ourselves in swamps and mountains so inaccessible that we can be neither discovered nor taken.

Our opponents, however, can neither pursue anybody, by reason of their heavy armour, nor yet flee; and if they ever do slip away from us, they take refuge in certain appointed spots, where they shut themselves up as in a trap. But these are not the only respects in which they are vastly inferior to us: There is also the fact that they cannot bear up under hunger, thirst, cold, or heat, as we can. They require shade and covering, they require kneaded bread and wine and oil, and if any of these things fails them, they perish; for us, on the other hand, any grass or root serves as bread, the juice of any plant as oil, any water as wine, any tree as a house. Furthermore, this region is familiar to us and is our ally, but to them it is unknown and hostile. As for the rivers, we swim them naked, whereas they do not get across them easily even with boats. Let us, therefore, go against them trusting boldly to good fortune. Let us show them that they are hares and foxes trying to rule over dogs and wolves.'

When she had finished speaking, she employed a species of divination letting a hare escape from the fold of her dress; and since it ran in what they considered the auspicious side, the whole multitude shouted with pleasure, and Boudicca, raising her hand towards heaven, said: 'I thank thee; Andraste, and call upon thee as woman speaking to woman; for I rule over no burden-bearing Egyptians as did Nitocris, nor over trafficking Assyrians as did Semiramis (for we have by now gained thus much learning from the Romans!), much less over the Romans themselves as did Messalina once and afterwards Agrippina and now Nero (who, though in name a man, is in fact a woman, as is proved by his singing, lyre-playing and beautification of his person); nay, those over whom I rule are Britons, men that know not how to till the soil or ply a trade, but are thoroughly versed in the art of war and hold all things in common, even children and wives, so that the latter possess the same value as the men. As the queen, then, of such men and of such women, I supplicate and pray thee for victory, preservation of life, and liberty against men insolent, unjust, insatiable, impious, – if, indeed, we ought to term those people men who bathe in warm water, eat artificial dainties, drink unmixed wine, anoint themselves with myrrh, sleep on soft couches with boys for bedfellows – boys past their prime at that, – and are slaves to a lyre-player and a poor one too.

Wherefore may this Mistress Domiyia-Nero reign no longer over me or over you men; let the wench sing and lord it over Romans, for they surely deserve to be the slaves of such a woman after having submitted to her so long. But for us, Mistress, be thou alone ever our leader.'

Tacitus's account in the Agricola, of the beginning of the rebellion, with a speech which is unattributed

For the Britons, freed from their repressions by the absence of the dreaded legate, began to discuss the woes of slavery, to compare their wrongs and sharpen their sting in the telling. 'We gain nothing by submission except heavier burdens for willing shoulders. Once each tribe had one king, now two are clamped on us – the legate to wreak his fury on our lives, the procurator on our property. We subjects are damned in either case, whether our masters quarrel or agree. Their gangs of centurions or slaves, as the case may be, mingle violence and insult. Nothing is any longer safe from their greed and lust. In war it is the braver who takes the spoil; as things stand with us, it is mostly cowards and shirkers that rob our homes, kidnap our children and conscript our men. Any cause is good enough for us to die for – any but our country's. But what a mere handful our invaders are, if we reckon up our own numbers. The Germans, reckoning so, threw off the yoke, and they had only a river, not the Ocean, to shield them. We have country, wives and parents to fight for, the Romans have nothing but greed and self-indulgence. Back they will go, as the deified Julius went back, if only we can rival the valour of our fathers. We must not be scared by the loss of one battle or even two; success may foster the spirit of offence, but it is suffering that gives the power to endure.

The gods themselves are at last showing mercy to us Britons in keeping the Roman general away, with his army exiled in another island. For ourselves we have already taken the most difficult step – we have begun to plot. And in an enterprise like this there is more danger in being caught plotting than in taking the plunge.'

Dio's gruesome account of the sacking of Camulodunum and Londinium

Having finished an appeal to her people of this general tenor, Boudicca led her army against the Romans; for these chanced to be without a leader, inasmuch as Paulinus, their commander, had gone on an expedition to Mona, an island near Britain. This enabled her to sack and plunder two Roman cities, and, as I have said, to wreak indescribable slaughter. Those who were taken captive by the Britons were subjected to every known form of outrage. The worst and most bestial atrocity committed by their captors was the following. They hung up naked the noblest and most distinguished women and then cut off their breasts and sewed them to their mouths, in order to make the victims appear to be eating them; afterwards they impaled the women on sharp skewers run lengthwise through the entire body. All this they did to the accompaniment of sacrifices, banquets and wanton behaviour, not only in all their other sacred places, but particularly in the grove of Andate. This was their name for Victory, and they regarded her with most exceptional reverence.

Dio's account of Suetonius Paulinus's exhortation speech to his troops, before the 'big' battle

While ordering and arranging his men he also exhorted them, saying: 'Up, fellow-soldiers! Up Romans! Show these accursed wretches how far we surpass them even in the midst of evil fortune. It would be shameful, indeed, for you to lose ingloriously now what but a short time ago you won by your valour. Many a time, assuredly, have both we ourselves and our fathers, with far fewer numbers than we have at present, conquered far more numerous antagonists. Fear not, then, their numbers or their spirit of rebellion; for their boldness rests on nothing more than headlong rashness unaided by arms or training. Neither fear them because they have burned a couple of cities; for they did not capture them by force nor after a battle, but one was betrayed and the other abandoned to them. Exact from them now, therefore, the proper penalty for these deeds, and let them learn by actual experience the difference between us, whom they have wronged, and themselves.'

After addressing these words to one division he came to another and said: 'Now is the time, fellow-soldiers, for zeal, now is the time for daring. For if you show yourselves brave men today, you will recover all that you have lost; if you overcome these foes, no one else will any longer withstand us. By one such battle you will both make your present possessions secure and subdue whatever remains; for everywhere our soldiers, even though they are in other lands, will emulate you and foes will be terror-stricken. Therefore, since you have it within your power either to rule all mankind without a fear, both the nations that your fathers left to you and those that you yourselves have gained in addition, or else to be deprived of them altogether, choose to be free, to rule, to live in wealth, and to enjoy prosperity, rather than, by avoiding the effort, to suffer the opposite of all this.'

After making an address of this sort to these men, he went on to the third division, and to them he said: 'You have heard what outrages these damnable men have committed against us, nay more, you have even witnessed some of them. Choose, then, whether you wish to suffer the same treatment yourselves as our comrades have suffered and to be driven out of Britain entirely, besides, or else by conquering to avenge those that have perished and at the same time furnish to the rest of mankind an example, not only of benevolent clemency toward the obedient, but also of inevitable severity towards the rebellious. For my part, I hope, above all, that victories will be ours; first, because the gods are our allies (for they almost always side with those who have been wronged); second, because of the courage that is our heritage, since we are Romans and have triumphed over all mankind by our valour; next, because of our experience (for we have defeated and subdued these very men who are now arrayed against us); and lastly, because of our prestige (for those with us whom we are about to engage are not antagonists, but our slaves, whom we conquered even when they were free and independent). Yet if the outcome should prove contrary to our hope, – for I will not shrink from mentioning even this possibility, – it would be better for us to fall fighting bravely than be captured and impaled, to look upon our own entrails cut from our bodies, to be spitted on red-hot skewers, to perish by being melted in boiling water – in a word, to suffer as though we had been thrown to lawless and impious wild beasts. Let us, therefore, either conquer them or die on the spot. Britain will be a noble monument for us, even though all the other Romans here should be driven out; for in any case our bodies shall for ever possess this land.'

After addressing these and like words to them he raised the signal for battle.

Boudicca's speech to the British tribes before the 'big' battle, as proffered by Tacitus in his Annals

Boudicca drove round all the tribes in a chariot with her daughters in front of her.

'We British are used to woman commanders in war,' she cried. 'I am descended from mighty men! But now I am not fighting for my kingdom and wealth. I am fighting as an ordinary person for my lost freedom, my bruised body, and my outraged daughters. Nowadays Roman rapacity does not even spare our bodies. Old people are killed, virgins raped. But the gods will grant us the vengeance we deserve! The Roman division which dared to fight is annihilated. The others cower in their camps, or watch for a chance to escape. They will never face even the din and roar of all our thousands, much less the shock of our onslaught. Consider how many of you are fighting – and why. Then you will win this battle, or perish. That is what I, a woman, plan to do! – let the men live in slavery if they will.'

Suetonius Paulinus's appeal to his troops before the 'big' battle, as reported by Tacitus, in the Annals

Suetonius trusted his men's bravery. Yet he too, at this critical moment, offered encouragement and appeals. 'Disregard the clamours and empty threats of the natives!' he said. 'In their ranks, there are more women than fighting men. Unwarlike, unarmed, when they see the arms and courage of the conquerors who have routed them so often, they will break immediately. Even when a force contains many divisions, few among them win the battle – what special glory for your small numbers to win the renown of a whole army! Just keep in close order. Throw your javelins, and then carry on: use shield-bosses to fell them, swords to kill them. Do not think of plunder. When you have won, you will have everything.'

Bibliography

Dio Cassius (trans. Earnest Cary), *Roman History*, Loeb Classical Library, Harvard University Press

Hall, David and Coles, John, *The Fenland Survey 1994*, English Heritage

Julius Caesar (trans. S A Handford), *The Conquest of Gaul*, Penguin Classics

Margary, Ivan D, *Roman Roads in Britain*, Baker, 1967

Suetonius (trans. Robert Graves), *The Twelve Caesars*, Penguin Classics

Tacitus (trans. Kenneth Wellesley), *The Histories*, Penguin Classics

—— (trans. H Mattingly), *On Britain and Germany*, Penguin Classics

—— (trans. Michael Grant), *The Annals of Imperial Rome*, Penguin Classics

University of Exeter, *The Saxon Shore*, 1989

Wacher, John, *Roman Britain*, Dent, 1978

Webster, Graham, *Boudicca*, Batsford, 1978

Willson, Beckles (rev. edn by W J Wiltshire), *Lost England*, Hodder & Stoughton

Index